This Field Guide belongs to:

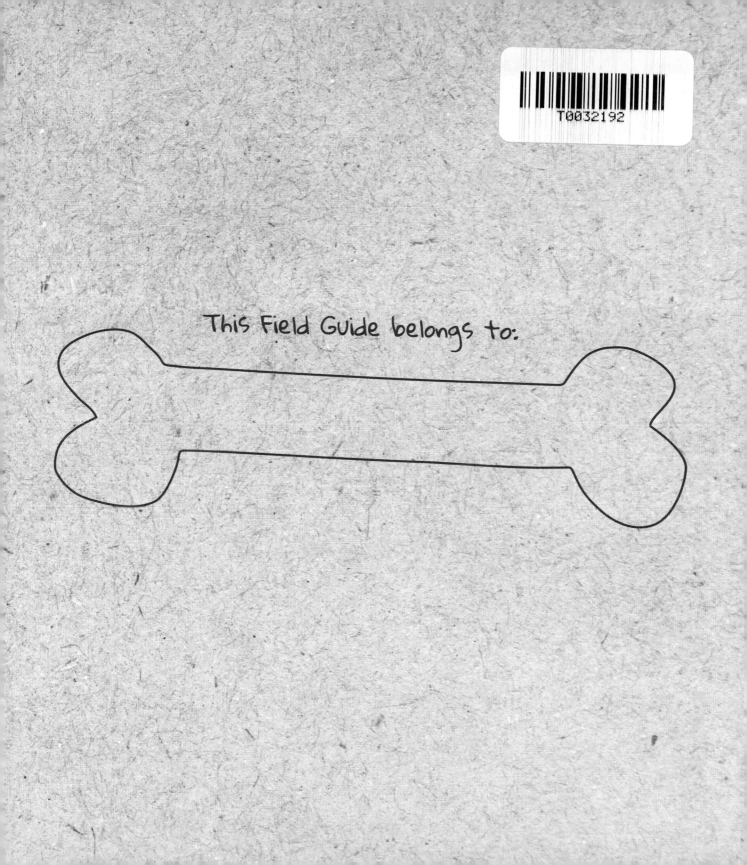

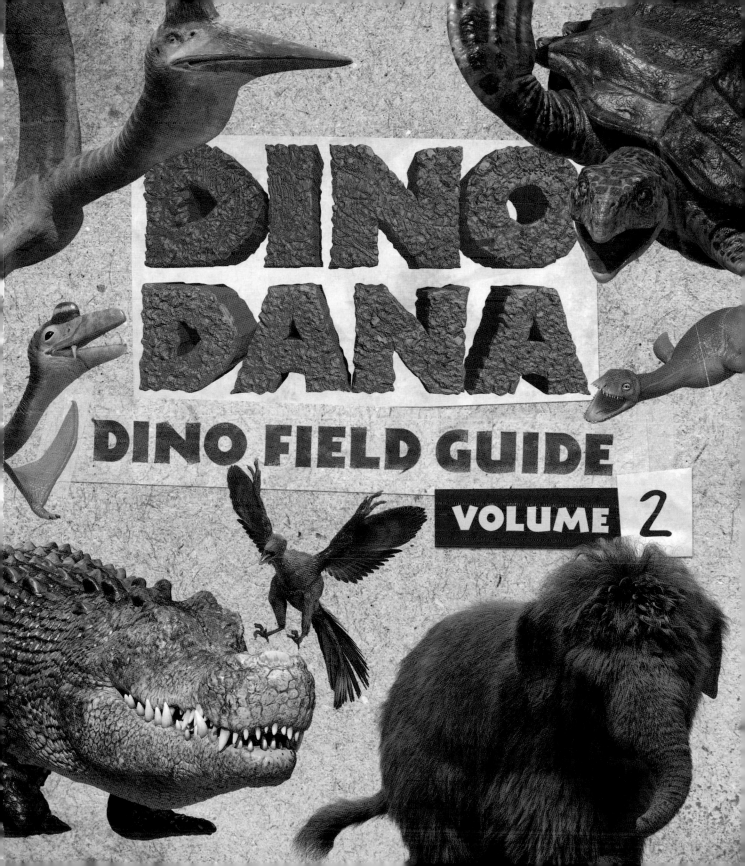

DINO DANA

DINO FIELD GUIDE

VOLUME 2

DINO DANA

DINO FIELD GUIDE

VOLUME 2

J.J. Johnson, Christin Simms &
Colleen Russo Johnson, PhD

mango
PUBLISHING GROUP

CORAL GABLES

Cover Design: Sinking Ship Entertainment

Interior Book Design: Jason Lean

Published by Mango Publishing, an imprint of Mango Media Inc.

For permission requests, please contact the publisher at:

Mango Publishing Group
2850 Douglas Road, 2nd Floor
Coral Gables, FL 33134 USA
info@mango.bz

For special orders, quantity sales, course adoptions and corporate sales, please email the publisher at sales@mango.bz. For trade and wholesale sales, please contact Ingram Publisher Services at customer.service@ingramcontent.com or +1.800.509.4887.

Dino Dana: Dino Field Guide Volume 2: Pterosaurs and Other Prehistoric Creatures!

ISBN: (p) 978-1-64250-521-4 (e) 978-1-64250-522-1

BISAC: JNF037050, JUVENILE NONFICTION / Science & Nature / Fossils

LCCN: 2020945288

ACKNOWLEDGEMENTS

PALEONTOLOGIST CONSULTANTS

Dr. Victoria Arbour ← *Her favorite prehistoric creature is the Pterodaustro because she thinks their teeth are really weird and interesting!* → *I agree!*

Dr. David Evans ← *His favorite is the Titanoboa!*

Dr. Donald Henderson ← *He can't decide between the Quetzalcoatlus and the Titanboa because they are both so BIIIG!*

FOR SINKING SHIP ENTERTAINMENT

Matt Bishop, J.J. Johnson, Blair Powers, Partners

Kate Sanagan and Marilyn Kynaston, Heads of Sales and Distribution

Jason Lean, Book Designer

Special thanks to Alexis Grieve, Holden Mohring, Daniel Rose, Tara Tote, Sarah Tung, Gavin Friesen and Courtney Lee

All dinosaur designs and artwork designed in house by the Sinking Ship Entertainment VFX team.

Photograph "Fish-in-a-fish" on page 23 courtesy of The Sternberg Museum of Natural History.

DEDICATION

To Lois Johnson, Maureen & Andy Russo, and all the parents who delight in their kids' imaginings. Thank you for unlocking the magic of the everyday!

Endless love and appreciation from your son, daughter, grandchildren (Ripley & Rex) and fur grandchildren (Charlie and Lambert)

To Casey, I'm so so so excited to be your aunt and I can't wait to help your mom and dad show you the world (cue Uncle Adam singing). To Ripley and Rex, being your aunt is a total joy, thank you for making every video call a dino adventure (I hope that continues into your twenties).

Love you all, Aunt Chris/Simms

INTRODUCTION

My name is DANA and I (LOVE) dinosaurs.

Because they're **BIG** and **CUTE** and **SCARY** and **FUN**.

BUT I also love other prehistoric creatures like pterosaurs, marine reptiles, and early mammals. Which is why I made a field guide just for them!

Because when I grow up, I want to be a paleontologist and paleontologists don't just study dinos.

Really?!?!

YES REALLY! A paleontologist is a

scientist who studies the history of life on Earth through fossils.

Like bones that have been dug up.

Dinosaurs aren't the only creatures that left fossils for us to discover: so did other prehistoric animals and plants. And if we can learn about them, we can understand ALL life better.

including dinosaurs!

And that's the job of a paleontologist, to learn about life so we can understand how we fit into everything.

YOU and ME

Which is also why we need to keep asking QUESTIONS!

We need to ask questions about what we KNOW, what we thought we KNEW, and what we THINK the answer might be.

SO MANY QUESTIONS!!

Hopefully my second Dino Field Guide will help you answer some of

your QUESTIONS and help you come up with entirely NEW ONES.

Because that's our job, fellow
paleontologist-in-training!

11

Now start questioning!

Dana

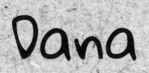

HOW TO USE MY FIELD GUIDE

Here are some tips to help you use my field guide for your own dino experiments.

STICKERS!

These make it easier to know which group each creature belongs to:

And what they like to eat:

 Pterosaurs

 Flying Dinosaurs

 Prehistoric Marine Creatures

 Prehistoric Mammals

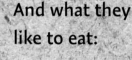 **Carnivore** **Herbivore**

 Terror Birds

 Prehistoric Snakes

 Prehistoric Insects

 Insectivore

TIMELINE

This shows you when each creature lived.

318 Million	299 Million	252 Million	201 Million	
PENNSYL-VANIAN	PERMIAN	TRIASSIC	JURASSIC	

SIZE CHART!

This shows how big each creature is compared to me. I'm probably about the same size as you.

Me vs. Mammoth

WHERE WE FOUND THEM

This map shows where each creature's fossils were first discovered.

Pterosaurs lived until 66 million years ago, but the mammoths were still around only 4,000 years ago.

Which means mammoths and people lived together for thousands of years!

US

| CRETACEOUS | 66 Million | PALEOGENE | 23 Million | NEOGENE | 2.6 Millio | QUATE |

PREHISTORIC TIMELINE EXPLANATION

Picture time like this Brachiosaurus:

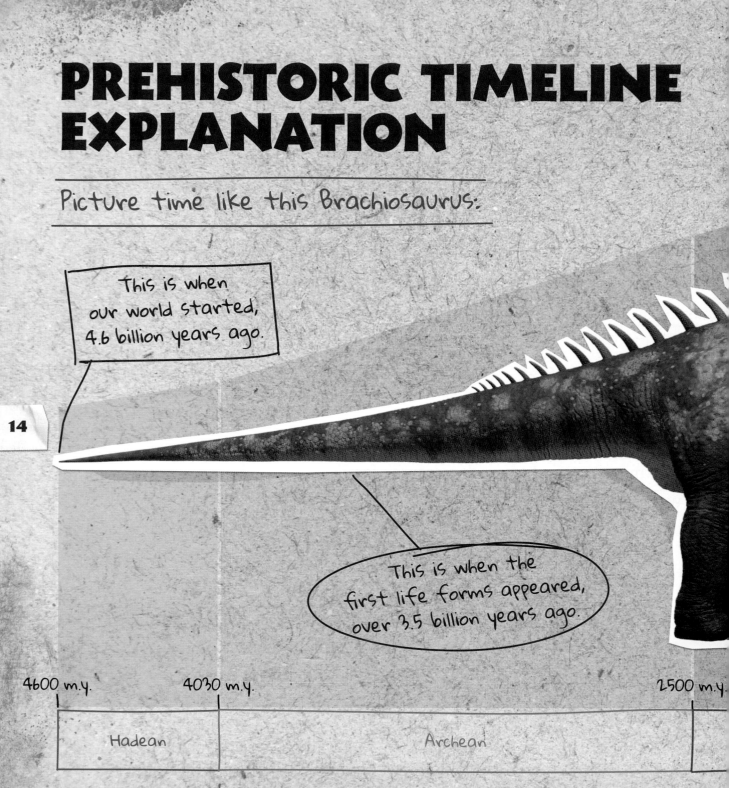

This is when our world started, 4.6 billion years ago.

This is when the first life forms appeared, over 3.5 billion years ago.

4600 m.y.	4030 m.y.		2500 m.y.
Hadean		Archean	

m.y. = million years

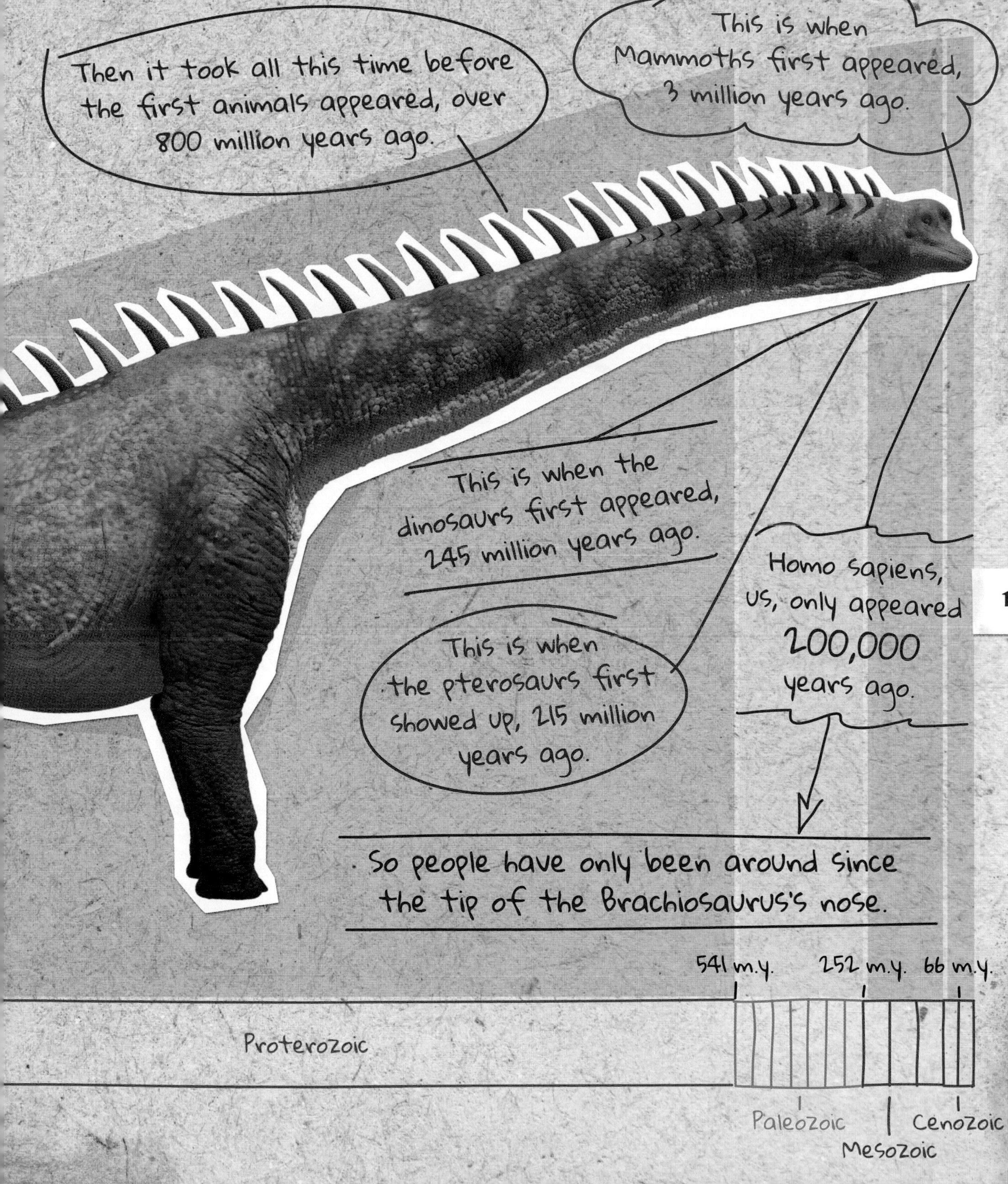
Then it took all this time before the first animals appeared, over 800 million years ago.
This is when Mammoths first appeared, 3 million years ago.
This is when the dinosaurs first appeared, 245 million years ago.
Homo sapiens, us, only appeared 200,000 years ago.
This is when the pterosaurs first showed up, 215 million years ago.
So people have only been around since the tip of the Brachiosaurus's nose.
541 m.y.
252 m.y.
66 m.y.
Proterozoic
Paleozoic
Mesozoic
Cenozoic

LEARN SOMETHING NEW

First Triassic
When the di-nos began
E-O-RAP-TOR
PRO-COMP-SONG-NA-THUS
And you just learned
something new.

Eoraptor

Procompsognathus

Proceratosaurus

Bellusaurus

Let's keep going with BELL-U-SAURUS
and PRO-CER-A-TO-SAUR-US

Then there's AM-IG-DAL-OH-DON
and EWE-STREP-TOE-SPON-DIE-LUSS

Amygdalodon

Eustrepospondylus

This song helped my seester Saara remember the dino timelines!

Two hundred and fifty-two million years ago is when the Age of Dinosaurs began
And it all makes sense somehow, when you know their time span
And then your test will be easy.

Next Jurassic
Way more di-no friends
DIP-LO-DOC-US
BRACH-I-O-SAUR-US
And you, just learned something new.

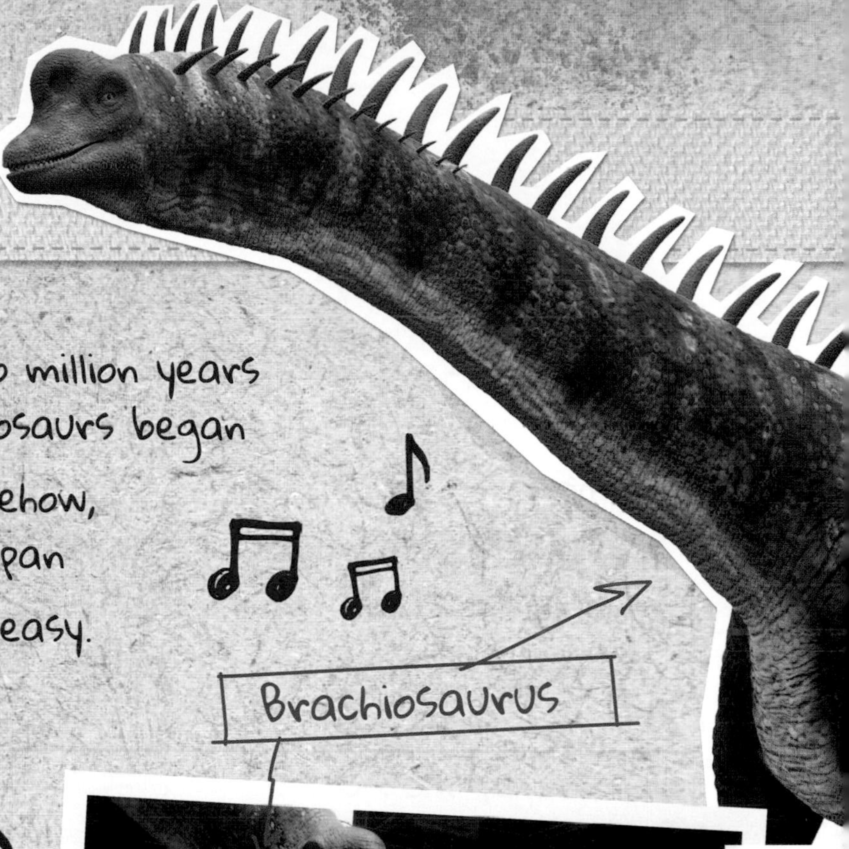

Brachiosaurus

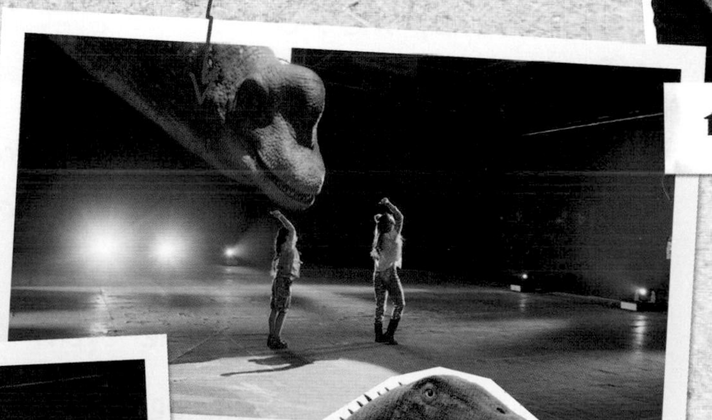

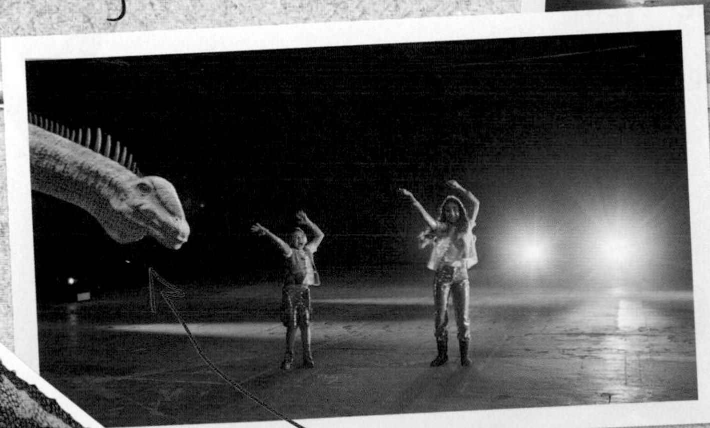

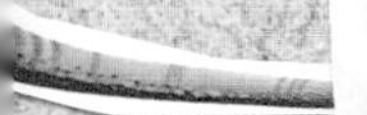

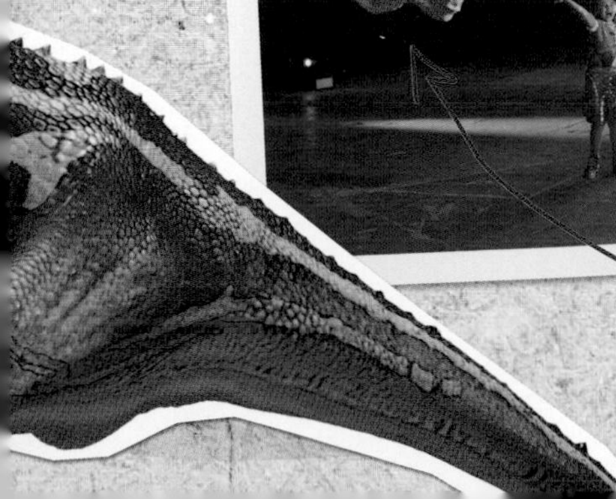

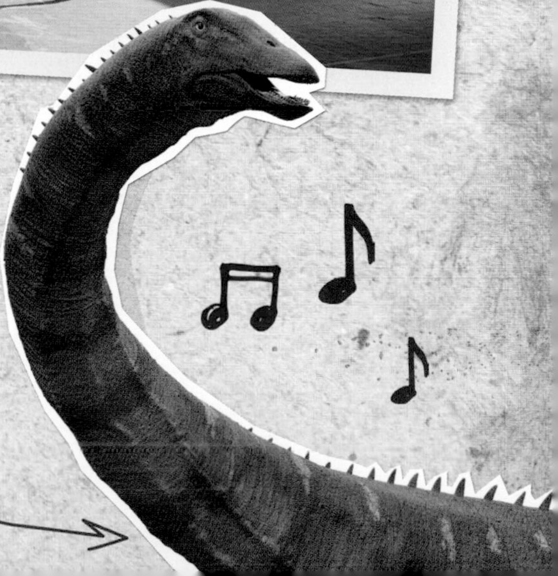

Diplodocus

@zraptor

Stegosaurus

You know this one,
it's a... OZ-RAP-TOR.
And over there is a... ?
STEG-OSAUR-US

Good! Now what about
this friend, she's a... ?
KEN-TRO-SAUR-US.

Over two hundred and one million
years ago is when the Jurassic began
And it all makes sense somehow
when you know their time span
And then my test will be easy.

Kentrosaurus

Triceratops

Euoplocephalus

Now Cretaceous
Last for the di-no-saurs
TRI-CER-A-TOPS
EUO-PLO-CEPH-A-LUS
And you just learned something new
And now, the Tyrannosaurus Rex!

One hundred and forty-five million years
ago is when the Cretaceous began
And it all makes sense somehow,
when I know their time span
And now your test will be easy.

First...Triassic
Then came the...Jurassic
Last was...Cretaceous
Now you know them all
'Cause you, just taught
me something new.

Tyrannosaurus Rex

WHAT DID THE WORLD LOOK LIKE?

Today, our world looks like this:

21ST Century

But millions of years ago when the dinosaurs and pterosaurs ruled the Earth, it looked like this:

Cretaceous Period

And millions of years before that, it looked like this:

called Pangea.

Which means "whole" because look at how all the continents were stuck together.

End of the Paleozoic Era

How did this... (**BUT**) ...become this?

Tectonic Plates

Tectonic plates are HUUUGE pieces of solid rock that our continents sit on.

These plates are constantly moving, just VEEERY slowly.

Tectonic plates move at the same speed that our toenails grow! As they shift they take the fossils buried deep inside them along for the ride!

How Do Dinosaurs and Prehistoric Creatures Become Fossils?

22

What is a fossil?

Checklist:
- ☐ From a prehistoric plant or animal.
- ☐ At least 10,000 years old.

Plant fossil

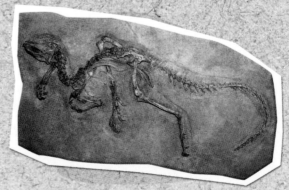

Animal fossil

Did you know there are different types of fossils?

Body Fossils comes directly from the animal.

Like bones and teeth.

Trace Fossils are evidence of animal activity.

Like footprints or DINO POOP!

Paleontologists call dino poop a COPROLITE. →

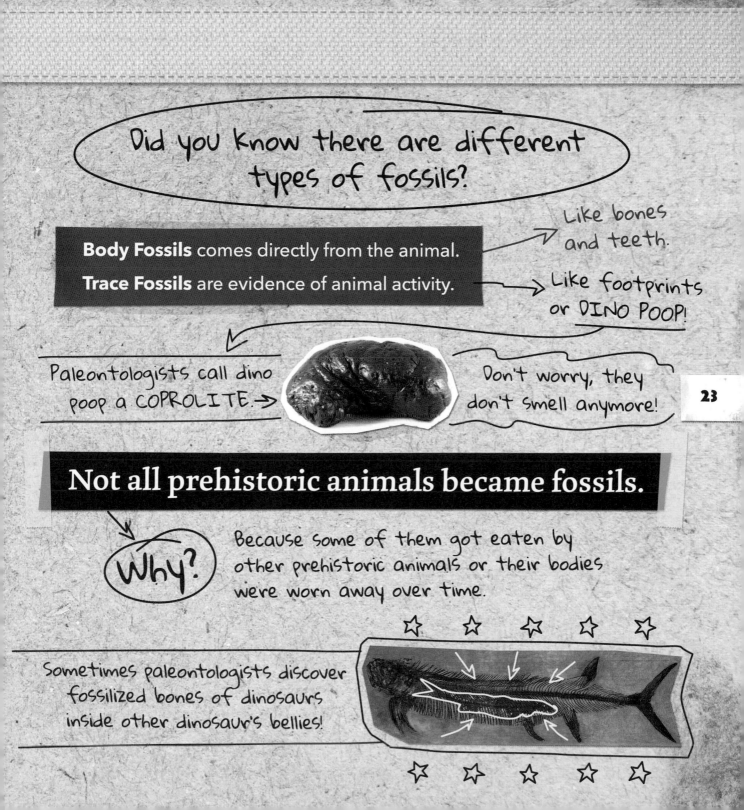

Don't worry, they don't smell anymore!

Not all prehistoric animals became fossils.

Why?

Because some of them got eaten by other prehistoric animals or their bodies were worn away over time.

Sometimes paleontologists discover fossilized bones of dinosaurs inside other dinosaur's bellies!

HOW?!?!

Step 1: A body gets buried under sand or mud.

Step 2: <u>Over time</u> the bones become rock like.

Like thousands of years.

BONE + MINERALS

BONE → ROCK

This is called petrification!

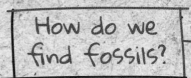

How do we find fossils? → BY DIGGING!

Over millions of years, the Earth's continents have changed shape. So parts that were once underwater are now up high!

This is why you can find fossils of prehistoric marine creatures at the tops of mountains!

FAMILY SIZE COMPARISON

A size comparison helps you see how big something is next to something else.

I compare prehistoric creatures to my family because it helps me imagine their sizes.

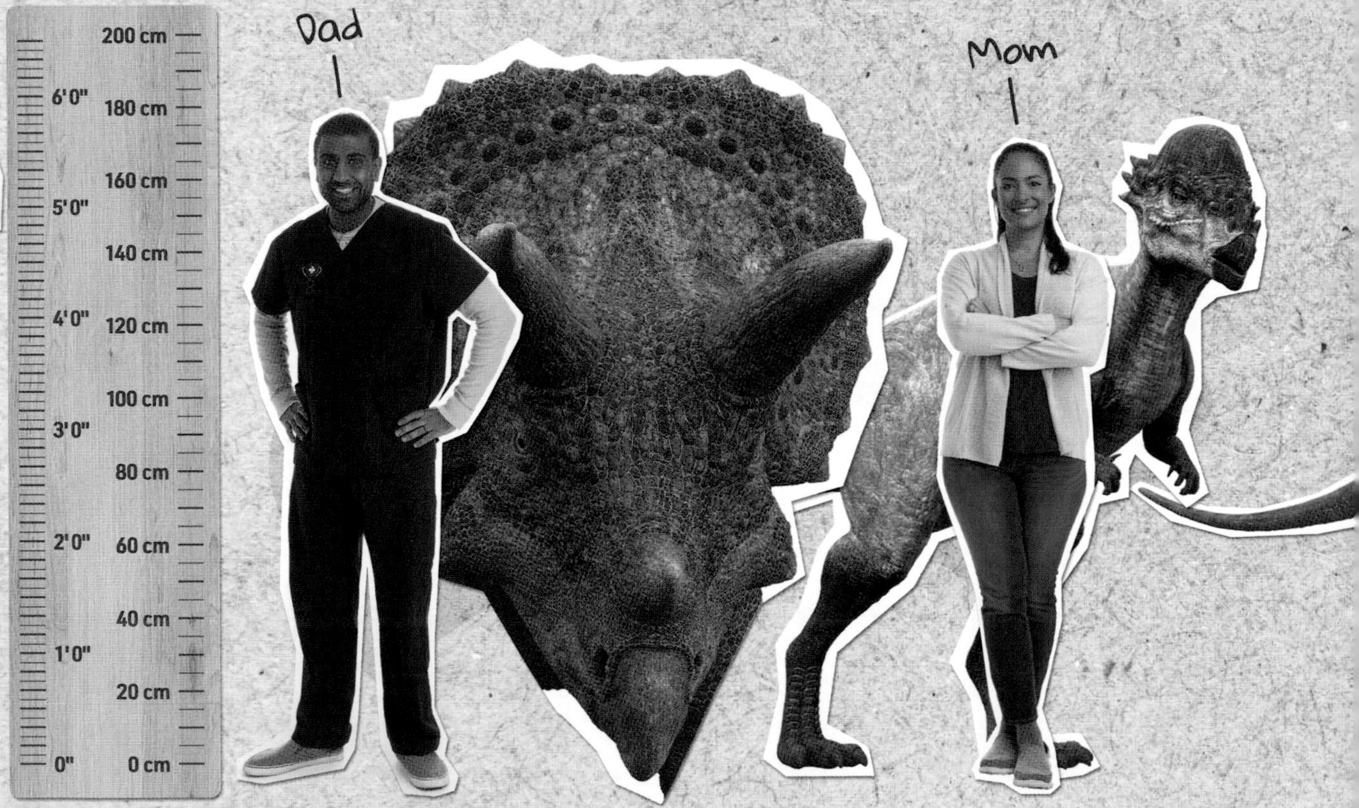

200 cm
6'0"
180 cm
160 cm
5'0"
140 cm
4'0"
120 cm
100 cm
3'0"
80 cm
2'0"
60 cm
40 cm
1'0"
20 cm
0"
0 cm
Dad
Mom

My family

Saara

Me

Therizinosaurus claw!

Dexter

Nixon

0"   1'0"   2'0"   3'0"   4'0"
0 cm   20 cm   40 cm   60 cm   80 cm   100 cm   120 cm   140 cm

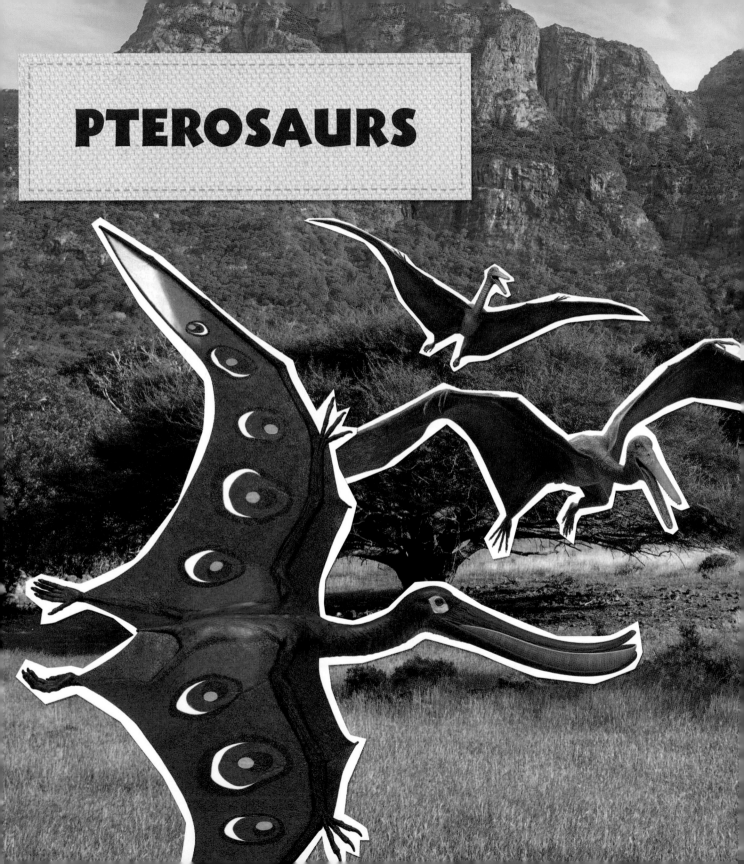

PTEROSAURS

PTEROSAURS

EXTINCT means they're not here anymore.

Pterosaurs lived with dinosaurs and went (extinct) around the same time, but they are not dinosaurs. They were flying reptiles. The word pterosaur even means "wing lizard."

30

Microraptor is a dinosaur.

But some dinosaurs have wings, so why aren't they pterosaurs?

Good question!

Evolved means when one thing, over time, changes to become another.

Birds today evolved from dinosaurs, not from pterosaurs.

T. Rex + Millions of Years = Chicken

How do we know?

Because bird and pterosaur wings are really different.

- Pterosaurs don't have feathers, instead they have stretched skin, like a sail.

- Pterosaur wings are made from one very long fourth finger.

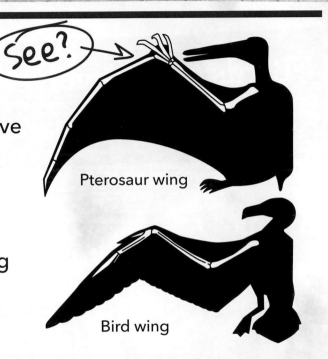

See?

Pterosaur wing

Bird wing

Pterosaur

Bird

Dinosaurs evolved into birds.

Pterosaurs evolved into... nothing.

↑

Which means they aren't alive anymore—except in our imaginations!

If it flies with feathery wings, it's a ➡ BIRD.

If it flies with leathery wings, it's a → PTEROSAUR.

PTERODACTYLUS

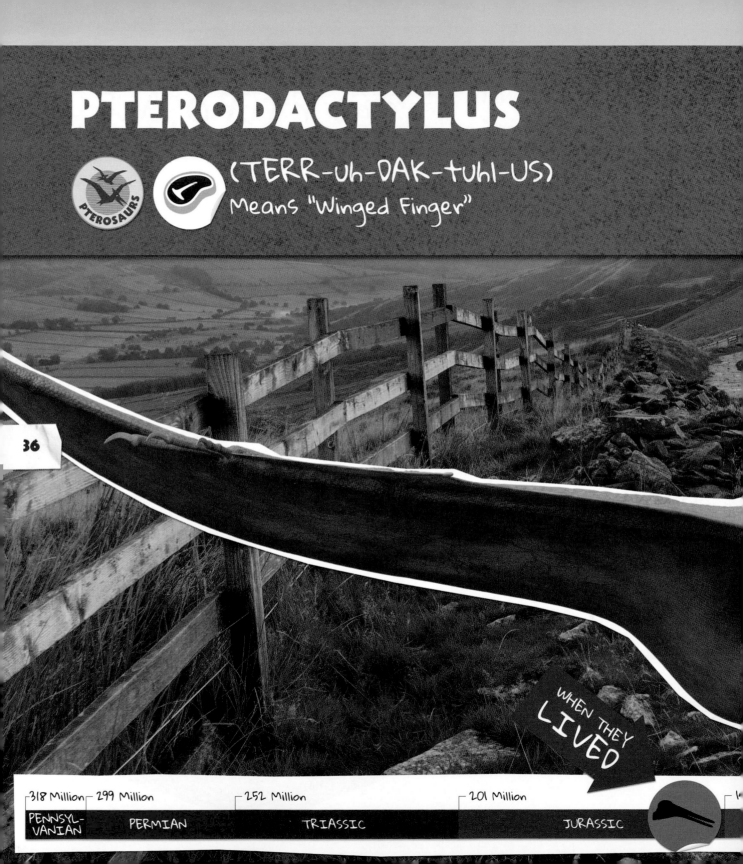

(TERR-uh-DAK-tuhl-US)
Means "Winged Finger"

PTEROSAURS

36

WHEN THEY LIVED

Found in
what is now
Europe.

37

US

BABY PTERODACTYLUS

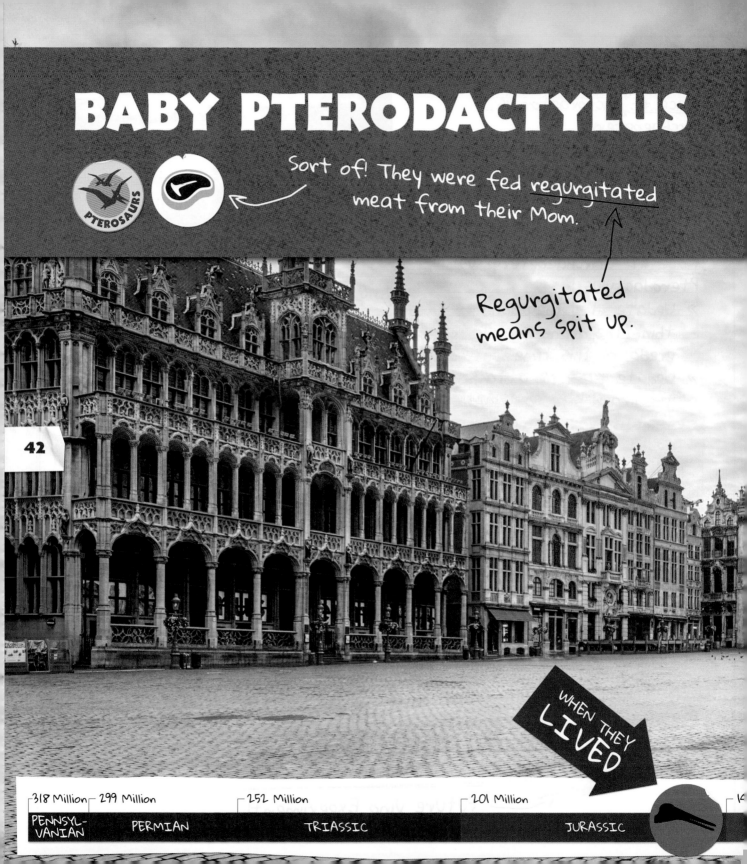

PTEROSAURS

Sort of! They were fed regurgitated meat from their Mom.

Regurgitated means spit up.

42

WHEN THEY LIVED

318 Million | 299 Million | 252 Million | 201 Million |

PENNSYL-VANIAN | PERMIAN | TRIASSIC | JURASSIC

Found in what is now Europe.

43

US

	66 Million	23 Million	2.6 Million
CRETACEOUS	PALEOGENE	NEOGENE	QUATERNARY

DINO EXPERIMENT ___614___

QUESTION: Why does the Pterodactylus push its babies out of the nest?

BACKGROUND RESEARCH NOTES:

Pterodactylus moms might have taken care of their babies until they could take care of themselves

Like most birds today

Finger   Leg

MY PLAN:

Observe a Pterodactylus nest.

FIELD NOTES:

Day 1: I found a baby Pterodactylus on the ground on my way to visit Mr. Hendrickson! She had fallen out of her nest. Poor baby Ptero.

← Mr. Hendrickson

FIELD NOTES (CONTINUED):

<u>Day 2</u> = I saw the mom Pterodactylus accidentally push the baby Ptero out of her nest! Mama Ptero needs to be more careful...

» Update #1 = I put the baby Ptero back in her nest.

» Update #2 = Mr. Hendrickson thinks the mom pushed the baby Ptero out on purpose! To help her leave the nest and learn to fly!

<u>Day 3</u> = This time on my bike ride I waited for the mama Ptero to push her baby out again.

» Update = Mr. Hendrickson was right! The baby started flying!

FINDING:

The mama Pterodactylus pushed her babies out of the nest to help them learn to fly. Sometimes you just need a little nudge from your mom.

PTERODAUSTRO

PTEROSAURS

(Tare-o-daw-stro)
Means "Wing from the South"

Found in what is now Chile!

48

318 Million	299 Million	252 Million	201 Million	1
PENNSYL-VANIAN	PERMIAN	TRIASSIC	JURASSIC	

49

WHEN THEY LIVED

US

	66 Million	23 Million	2.6 Million
...OUS	PALEOGENE	NEOGENE	QUATERNARY

PTERODAUSTRO

Their food was tiny invertebrates like krill.

Pterodaustro ate like flamingos today by filter feeding.

★ Weighed as much as a flamingo.

Filter feeding means it slurped up its food with water and sifted it through its hundreds of small teeth.

Had a very large skull.

Wings were as long as I am tall.

May have slept on water, like some ducks.

Me vs. Pterodaustro

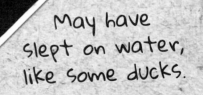

Sweet dreams Ducky!

DINO EXPERIMENT ___518___

QUESTION: How does the Pterodaustro protect itself from predators?

BACKGROUND RESEARCH NOTES:

★ The Pterodaustro looks like the flamingos Mr. Hendrickson is putting up in his yard!

★ Flamingos are birds and Pterodaustro are pterosaurs, but they could both fly!

A decoy is a fake animal scientists use for testing

MY PLAN:

Use a decoy Pterodaustro to see how Pterodaustro protected itself from predators.

FIELD NOTES:

1. I put my decoy next to Mr. Hendrickson's flamingos to see if a predator would attack.
   » Update = Oops. The Dromaeosaurus attacked Mr. Hendrickson's flamingos instead of my decoy Pterodaustro.

FIELD NOTES (CONTINUED):

2. I saw a real Pterodaustro fly away from the Dromaeosaurus. Flying away must be how they protect themselves!

3. I hung Mr. Hendrickson's flamingos up in the tree to protect them like a Pterodaustro protects itself—in the air away from predators!

» Update = The Dromaeosaurus climbed the tree to get to the flamingos! Uh oh. Too bad Mr. Hendrickson's flamingos can't actually fly!

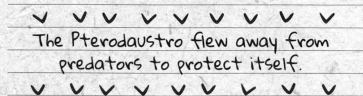

FINDING:

ⱽ ⱽ ⱽ ⱽ ⱽ ⱽ ⱽ ⱽ ⱽ

The Pterodaustro flew away from predators to protect itself.

ⱽ ⱽ ⱽ ⱽ ⱽ ⱽ ⱽ ⱽ ⱽ

Next time I'll use a flying decoy...

QUETZALCOATLUS

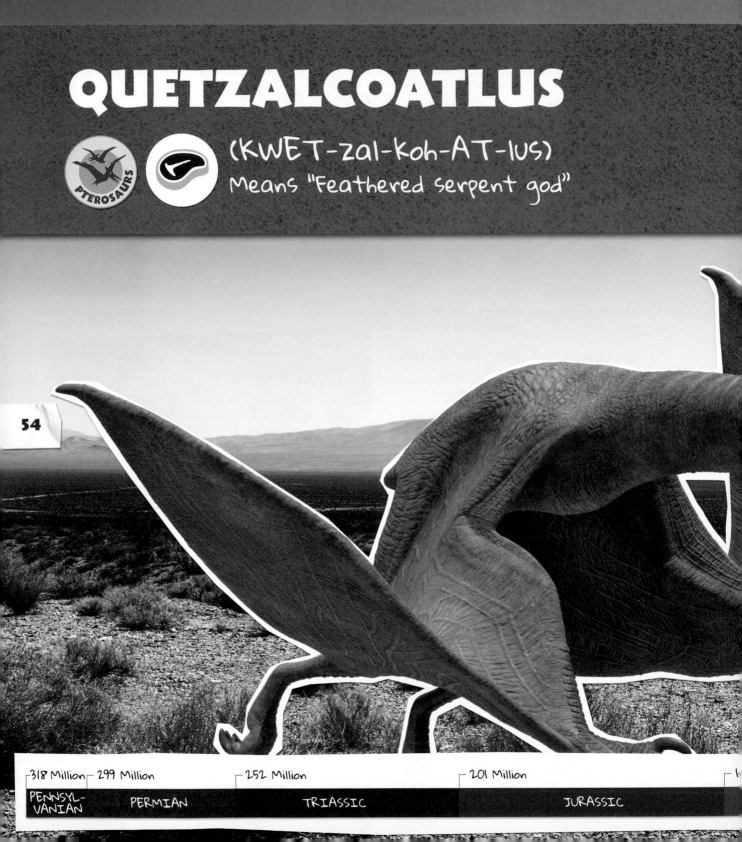

(KWET-zal-koh-AT-lus)
Means "Feathered serpent god"

PTEROSAURS

318 Million	299 Million	252 Million	201 Million	
PENNSYL-VANIAN	PERMIAN	TRIASSIC	JURASSIC	

Discovered in what is now Texas, USA.

WHEN THEY LIVED

CRETACEOUS		66 Million	23 Million	2.6 Million
		PALEOGENE	NEOGENE	QUATERNARY

US

QUETZALCOATLUS

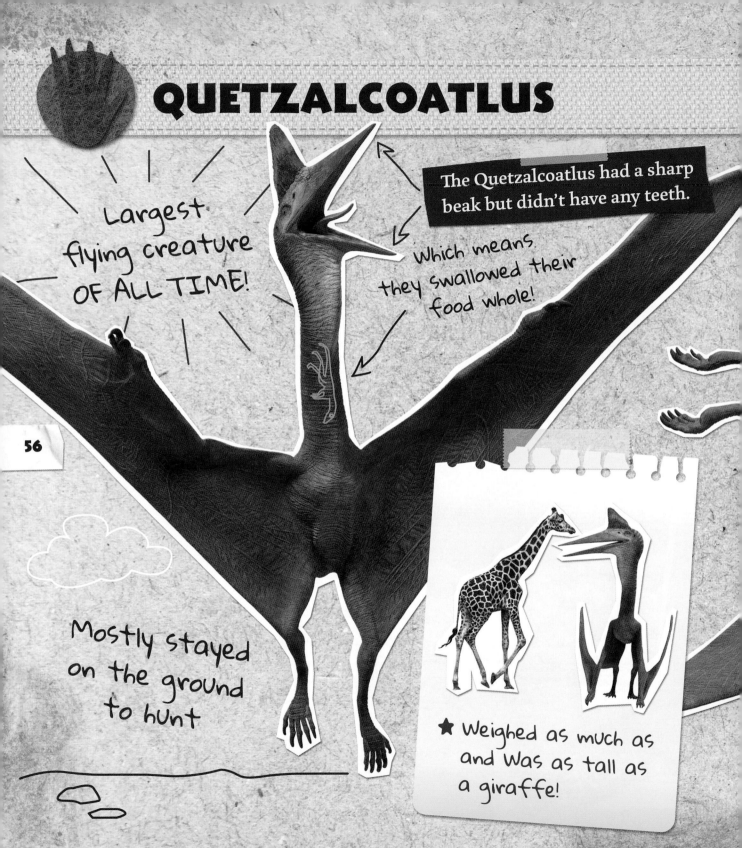

Largest flying creature OF ALL TIME!

The Quetzalcoatlus had a sharp beak but didn't have any teeth.

Which means they swallowed their food whole!

Mostly stayed on the ground to hunt

★ Weighed as much as and was as tall as a giraffe!

Only weighed as much as my dad!

~ Hunted small dinosaurs. ~

Had a super long neck, as long as three Saaras!!!

Could fly and glide.

Flap! Flap!

Weeee!

Me vs. Quetzalcoatlus

DINO EXPERIMENT **816**

QUESTION: Could the Quetzalcoatlus fly?

BACKGROUND RESEARCH NOTES:

★ The Quetzalcoatlus was the largest flying creature and largest Pterosaur of all time!

★ The Quetzalcoatlus may have hunted small dinosaurs and scavenged larger animals.

→ My friend Logan

★ I think it could fly, but my new friend Logan doesn't think it could.

MY PLAN:

Observe a Quetzalcoatlus in the museum with Logan!

FIELD NOTES:

1. The Quetzalcoatlus was hunting a Compsognathus, but didn't fly...

   » Update = That means the Quetzalcoatlus didn't fly to hunt, but it doesn't mean she <u>never</u> flew.

The experiment continues!

FIELD NOTES (CONTINUED):

2. Maybe the Quetzalcoatlus
   flew when she was being
   hunted! It's T. rex time!
   » Update #1 = The
     Quetzalcoatlus jumped off
     the railing and flew down
     to escape me!
   » Update #2 = Logan
     reminded me she could have ⟵
     just been gliding.

Flying is when you flap
your wings. Gliding is
when you ride the air.

3. Logan put on my T. rex
   backpack to chase the Quetz.
   His wheelchair was super fast!!!
   » Update = It worked, the
     Quetzalcoatlus flew away

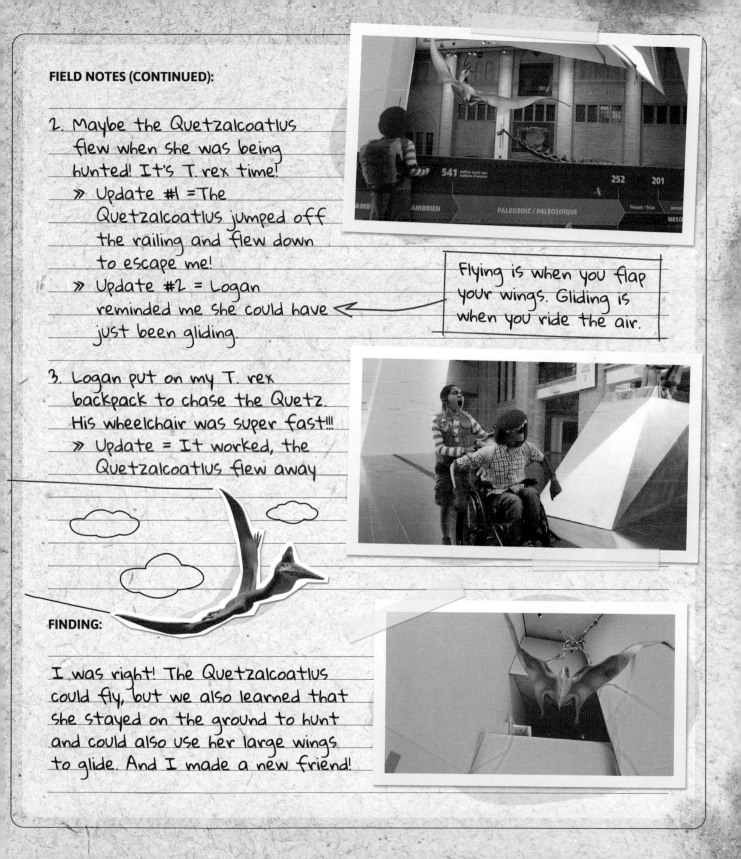

FINDING:

I was right! The Quetzalcoatlus
could fly, but we also learned that
she stayed on the ground to hunt
and could also use her large wings
to glide. And I made a new friend!

BABY
QUETZALCOATLUS

PTEROSAURS

↖ Quetzalcoatlus was first discovered in 1971!

60

318 Million	299 Million		252 Million		201 Million	
PENNSYL-VANIAN	PERMIAN		TRIASSIC		JURASSIC	

Discovered in what is now Texas, USA.

61

WHEN THEY LIVED

US

66 Million   23 Million   2.6 Million

CRETACEOUS   PALEOGENE   NEOGENE   QUATERNARY

DINO EXPERIMENT __901.5__ bonus experiment!

QUESTION: How does the Mama Quetzalcoatlus teach her babies to hunt?

BACKGROUND RESEARCH NOTES:

★ The Quetzalcoatlus was the biggest flying creature of all time, ever.

★ The Quetzalcoatlus may have built its nest on cliffs or mountains.

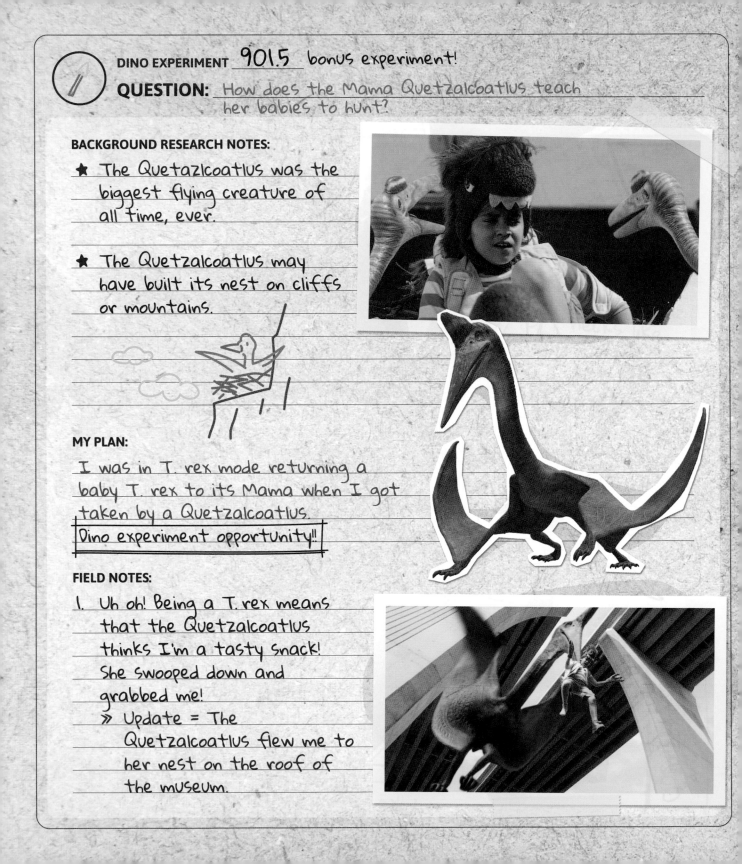

MY PLAN:

I was in T. rex mode returning a baby T. rex to its Mama when I got taken by a Quetzalcoatlus.
Dino experiment opportunity!!

FIELD NOTES:

1. Uh oh! Being a T. rex means that the Quetzalcoatlus thinks I'm a tasty snack! She swooped down and grabbed me!
   » Update = The Quetzalcoatlus flew me to her nest on the roof of the museum.

FIELD NOTES (CONTINUED):

2. The Quetzalcoatlus keeps pushing me toward her nest. I don't think she wants to eat me, I think <u>she</u> wants her <u>babies</u> to eat me!
   » Update = Oh no! Her babies hatched. Now I'm really in trouble.

3. I can't let the babies eat me! I have to do something.
   » Update #1 = The mama Quetzalcoatlus is the kind of mom who cuts up her babies' food. Yikes!
   » Update #2 = Saara and my friends Jadiel and Mateo came to save me! We all worked together and we got away!

FINDING:

The mama Quetzalcoatlus teaches her babies to hunt by bringing them live prey (like baby dinosaurs).

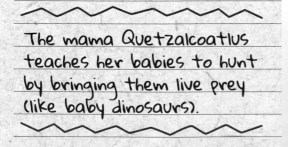

FLYING DINOSAURS

ARCHAEOPTERYX

(Ar-kee-OP-ter-ix)
Means "First Wing"

Because it was the first flying dinosaur which makes it the first bird!

FLYING DINOSAURS

WHEN THEY LIVED

318 Million	299 Million		252 Million		201 Million		1
PENNSYL-VANIAN	PERMIAN		TRIASSIC			JURASSIC	

Found in what is now Germany.

US

	66 Million	23 Million	2.6 Million
CRETACEOUS	PALEOGENE	NEOGENE	QUATERNARY

THEY WILL SURVIVE

Even though they're extinct
and they're fossilized Dinos
used to rule the Earth,
just check her Dino Field Guide.

We could spend so many
nights thinking how they
survived so long
How they grew strong
Or we could come up with a song

To get you on track
For a test you'll ace
Dinos with such unique parts that
they're not afraid of being chased

Psi-ttac-o-saur-us has tail quills
Zuul has a club, could break your knee

Remembering a cool
fact about each dino
helped Saara remember
their names!

I bet this would work
with Pterosaurs too!

Zuul

Watch out!!

Psittacosaurus

Herbivores so well protected they
can basically run free but that's not all,
there's way way more just look around now
Having horns helped some dinosaurs

Kos-mo had so many horns no
one would even try

Sty-gi ready to rumble
Dra-co charged with a battle cry
So that is why, they will survive

With sharp horns to scare off predators,
they know they'll stay alive

Kosmoceratops

Stygimoloch

77

Dracorex

Amargasaurus

Futalognkosaurus

Spikey smacks they have to give
Big boney frills that let them live
And they'll survive
They will survive, they will survive
But that's not all, there's way way more
Just look around now
Being huge helped some dinosaurs

A-marg-a-saurus neck went
right up to the sky

Stomp!

Stomp!

Saara

Me!

♫ ♪

♫

♫

Fu-ta makes the ground tremble
Quet-zal so big and could fly high
So that is why, they will survive
Just as long as they were really big,
they know they'll stay alive
Huge tail swipes they have to give
Or fly away so they can live
And they'll survive
They will survive!
They will survive!

Quetzalcoatlus

79

Amargasaurus

Futalognkosaurus

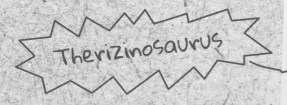

Therizinosaurus

PREHISTORIC MARINE CREATURES

DEINOSUCHUS

PREHISTORIC MARINE CREATURES

(DYI-noh-SOOK-us)
Means "Terrible Crocodile"

But it's actually more related to alligators than crocodiles.

Why?
Future Dino Experiment!

92

318 Million	299 Million	252 Million	201 Million	14
PENNSYL-VANIAN	PERMIAN	TRIASSIC	JURASSIC	

First discovered in what is now North Carolina, USA.

93

WHEN THEY LIVED

US

CRETACEOUS

66 Million
PALEOGENE

23 Million
NEOGENE

2.6 Million
QUATERNARY

DINO EXPERIMENT _509_

QUESTION: How did the Deinosuchus, Spinosaurus, and Pterodactylus get into the water?

BACKGROUND RESEARCH NOTES:

★ We're at the pool today and Saara has to jump off the high diving board to pass her swim course. But she's too scared to do it!

MY PLAN:

Observe how different prehistoric creatures got into the water to help Saara!

FIELD NOTES:

1. The Deinosuchus at the pool is getting into the water just like crocodiles today, by crawling in! I'll have Saara start by crawling down into the waterslide to get in like a Deinosuchus!

   » Update = She did it!

FIELD NOTES (CONTINUED):

2. The Spinosaurus mom and baby walked right into the pool! I'll have Saara walk into the water off of the low diving board like a confident Spinosaurus.

» Update = Another success!

3. Now, we need to get Saara off the high board. There's no dinosaur that would have dived into the water from that high though... Think, Dana, think....

» Update #1 = I've got it! A prehistoric winged reptile like the Pterodactylus would dive looking for fish to eat!

» Update #2 = Saara did it! She even squawked as she jumped off like a Pterodactylus!

FINDING:

The Deinosuchus would crawl into water, the Spinosaurus would walk into water, and the Pterodactylus would dive from up high into the water!

LIVYATAN

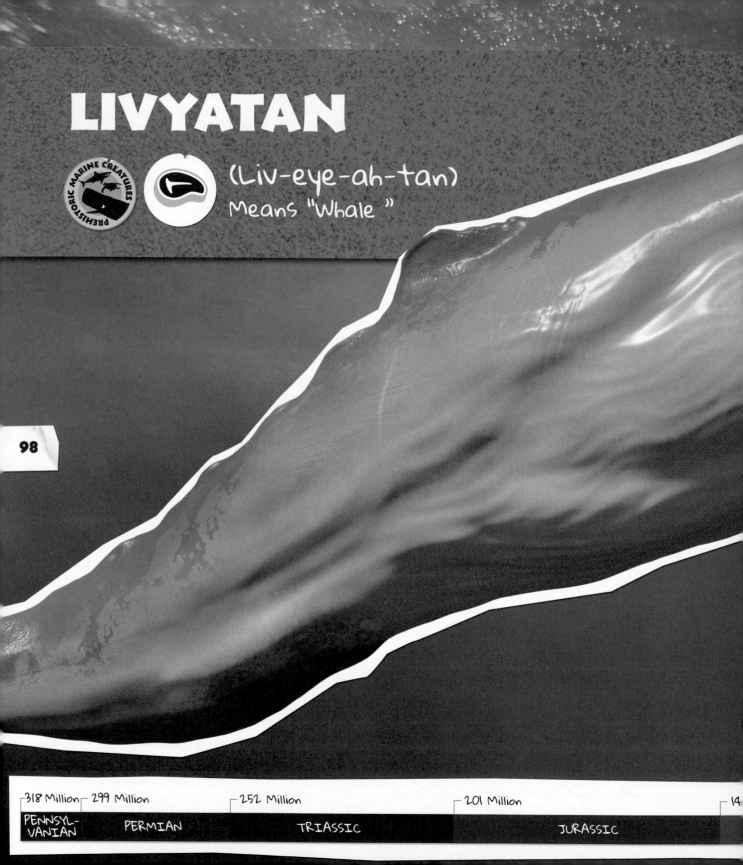

(Liv-eye-ah-tan)
Means "Whale"

98

Found in what
is now Peru.

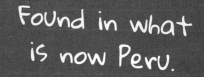

How did paleontologists
find a whale on land?
Because millions of years
ago, that part of the world
would have been underwater!

WHEN THEY
LIVED

US

	66 Million	23 Mi		2.6 Million
CRETACEOUS	PALEOGENE			QUATERNARY

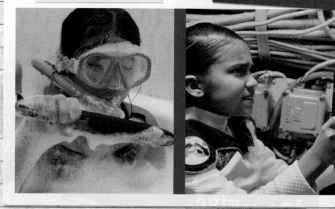

DINO EXPERIMENT __801__

QUESTION: Which prehistoric marine creature was the apex predator?

BACKGROUND RESEARCH NOTES: ← They're basically undefeatable!

★ Apex predators are animals that are so powerful that no other animal can eat them.

★ The Megalodon is the largest shark of all time! It's faster than the Livyatan and has a stronger bite.
  » It's ten times heavier than today's great white shark.

★ The Livyatan is about the same size as the Megalodon but with a much bigger mouth and massive teeth, which means a bigger bite.

MY PLAN:

Use my bathtub (and my imagination) to see the Megalodon take on the Livyatan...all from my very own submarine!

FIELD NOTES:

1. The Livyatan and Megalodon have spotted each other! But in my submarine I can't pilot and captain at the same time... I need back up!
   » Update = I convinced Saara to pilot the submarine!

FIELD NOTES (CONTINUED):

2. The Megalodon is going after the Livyatan! Will the Megaldon's speed be enough to get the Livyatan?

   » Update #1 = The Livyatan went after the Megalodon, but the Megalodon got away.

   » Update #2 = Now the Megalodon is coming toward us! We need backup in the engine room!

   » Update #3 = Time to get Engineer Dad!

3. Time to test which is better— the Livyatan's large teeth or the Megalodon's strong bite?

   » Update = The Livyatan won!!! She injured the Megalodon, and went to breach (jump out of the water) to show she's the boss!

FINDING:

The Livyatan is the apex predator! The Livyatan won out over the Megalodon. Large mouth and teeth for the win!

MEGALODON

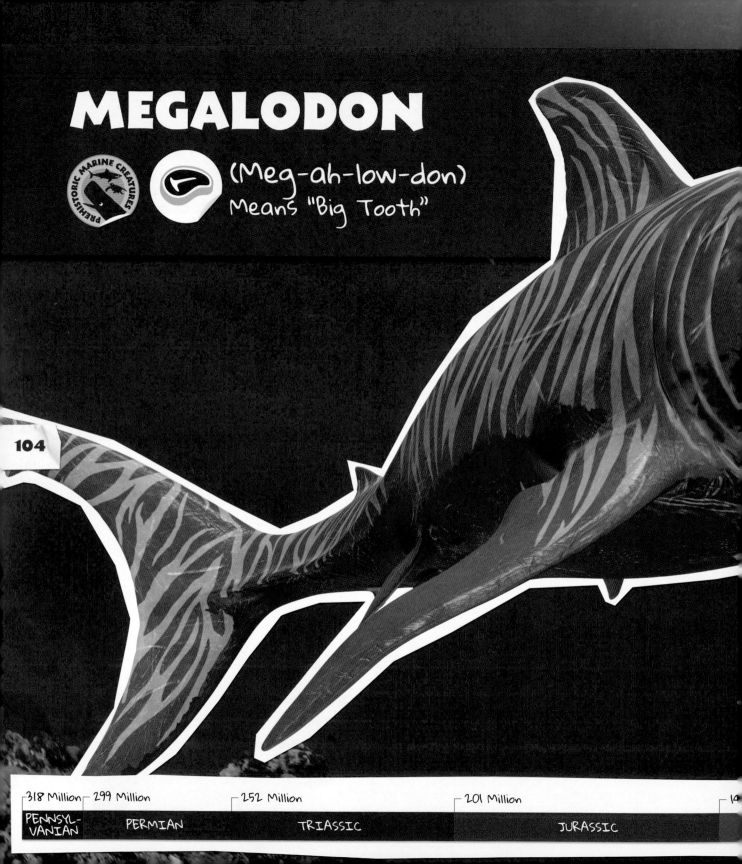

(Meg-ah-low-don)
Means "Big Tooth"

PREHISTORIC MARINE CREATURES

318 Million	299 Million	252 Million	201 Million	
PENNSYL-VANIAN	PERMIAN	TRIASSIC		JURASSIC

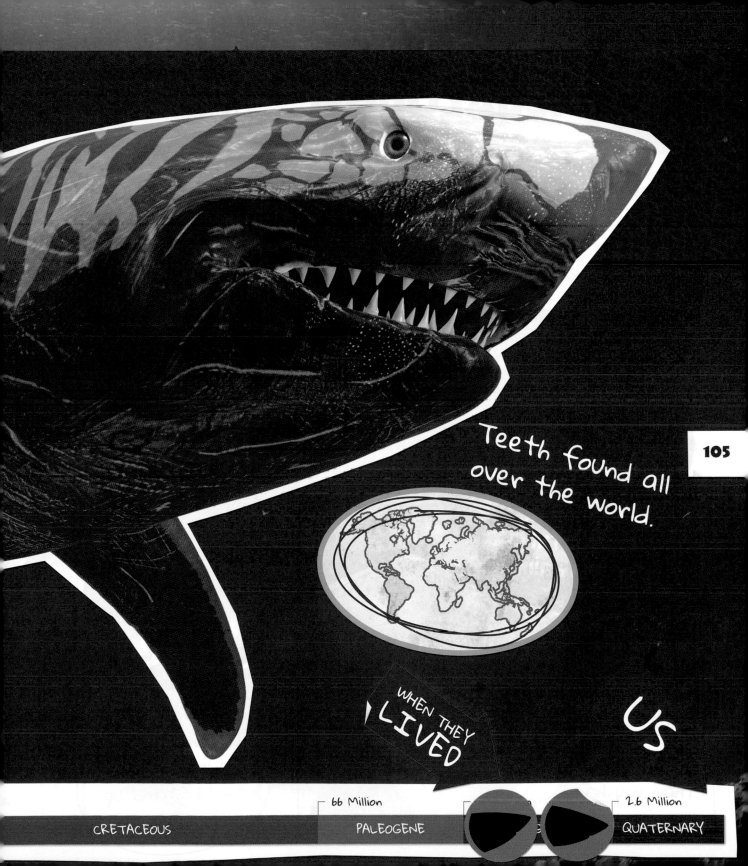

Teeth found all over the world.

WHEN THEY LIVED

US

CRETACEOUS	66 Million	PALEOGENE	2.6 Million	QUATERNARY

PLESIOSAUR

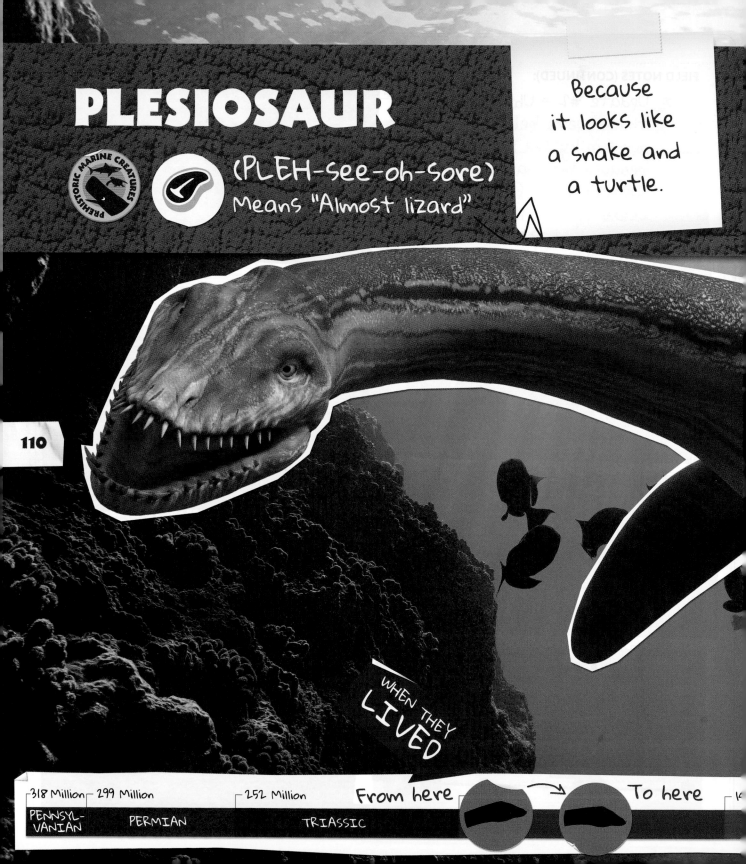

PREHISTORIC MARINE CREATURES

(PLEH-see-oh-sore)
Means "Almost lizard"

Because it looks like a snake and a turtle.

110

WHEN THEY LIVED

318 Million — 299 Million — 252 Million — From here — To here —

PENNSYL-VANIAN · PERMIAN · TRIASSIC

PLESIOSAUR

★ Weighed as much as a leatherback turtle—the heaviest turtle alive today.

Its neck was as long as two of my moms!!

Had four big flippers that helped them swim.

① ② ③ ④

Mary Anning was the first to discover an almost complete plesiosaur in 1820.

That's two hundred years ago!

Were **piscivorous** meaning they ate fish.

113

Might have used their long neck to sneak up on fish.

Had sharp teeth!

Me vs. Plesio

BABY PLESIOSAUR

PREHISTORIC MARINE CREATURES

Flew through the water like pigeons by flapping their front flippers to swim.

116

WHEN THEY LIVED

318 Million | 299 Million | 252 Million | From here | To here | 14

PENNSYL-VANIAN | PERMIAN | TRIASSIC

DINO EXPERIMENT __513__

QUESTION: What did prehistoric marine creatures sound like underwater?

BACKGROUND RESEARCH NOTES:

★ Prehistoric marine creatures lived around the same time as dinosaurs but lived in the water instead of on land.

★ Plesiosaurs are prehistoric marine creatures with super long necks and four flippers.

MY PLAN:

Riley and I will use our imaginations to go back in time in a submarine to listen to prehistoric marine creatures!

FIELD NOTES:

1. We're making different sounds but can't hear any coming back to us...

2. We hear something! It's coming from inside the sub!! In the torpedo tube!

   » Update = It's a baby plesiosaur!!! SO CUTE BUT we need to get this baby back to his mom!

FIELD NOTES (CONTINUED):

3. Oh no—a Deinosuchus, a prehistoric marine creature that eats small sea creatures, is outside the sub and wants to eat the baby plesiosaur!

   » Update = We were able to dive down and back up to escape him!

4. Now there's a Spinosaurus! It's a dino that can swim underwater and eat anything it gets its long snout and claws on... including our sub!

   » Update = The Spino is trying to bite our sub, and the Deinosuchus is back too!!

5. We have an idea! We can have the baby call out to his mom to come save us!

   » Update = It worked! Adult plesiosaurs are as long as a bus, and the group of them that came to the baby's rescue scared off the Spino and Deinosuchus! Mom and baby are back together!

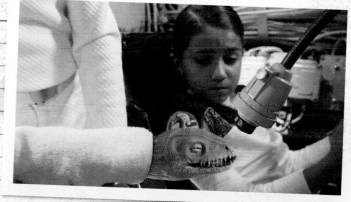

FINDING:

Plesiosaurs communicated underwater by calling out to each other! It sounds like squawks underwater!

SQUAWK!

SQUAWK!

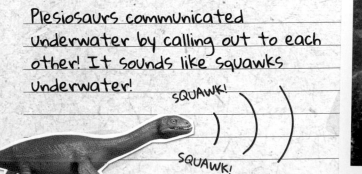

HOW DINOSAURS FIGHT

This is how dinosaurs fight
So they can, so they can
Beat their enemies and
save their lives
This is how dinosaurs fight

So they can, so they can
Eat their enemies with
their claw knives

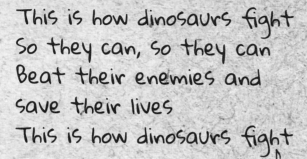

Nanuqsaurus

Di-nos!
Defending spree
They need some security
Di-nos!
Fight ability
So prey can't get away

Chomp Chomp!!

Hippodraco

Remembering how dinos fought each other helped Saara remember their names!

I bet that would work for Prehistoric Marine Creatures too!

Hipp-o-dra-co runs at you in herds oh no
Na-nuq-saur-us wants to bite your face oh no

Can you believe it?
Comp-sog-na-thus chases
you real fast oh no

123

Compsognathus

Maiasaura

Di-nos!
Defending spree
They need some security
Di-nos!
Fight ability
So prey can't get away

Mai-a-saur-a roar at you in groups oh no
Spi-no-saur-us tries to eat you whole oh no

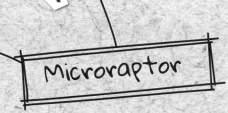

Microraptor

Can you believe it? ♪♫

Mi-cro-raptor goes quiet to flee oh no
You must escape!
'Cause dinos fight to
protect or eat you know! ♪ ♫

Spinosaurus

PREHISTORIC MAMMALS

PREHISTORIC MAMMALS

About the size of a mouse.

Prehistoric mammals first appeared 210 million years ago and started out super small. They lived in the shadows of the dinosaurs, and all mammals alive today are related to those first tiny mammals. ← Including you and me.

—— BUT ——
Over time mammals got a lot bigger like whales, lions, monkeys, dogs, and PEOPLE!

All mammals.

WHAT MAKES A MAMMAL A MAMMAL?

- All mammals are warm-blooded vertebrates.
- All mammals have hair or fur at some point.
- All mammals have mammary glands to feed their young.
- All mammals have a well-developed brain.

Warm-blooded means we can keep our temperature the same even when it's hot or cold outside.

Vertebrate means we have a backbone.

Even dolphins have a little hair on their chins!

Which means we're smart and can solve problems. Like how to get food.

Mammary glands are how mammals make milk for their babies.

Why were mammals so small for so long?

BECAUSE

When mammals and dinosaurs lived at the same time, dinos ate all the best food.

WHICH MEANS

Mammals couldn't grow very big.

BUT

When the dinosaurs went extinct, mammals took over and eventually became the biggest creatures on Earth.

Megafauna like the Brontotherium, Woolly Mammoth, and Smilodon became so large that they didn't have a lot of natural predators.

But around 10,000 years ago, most of the megafauna in North and South America disappeared.

131

Why? Maybe because it got colder or warmer, or because humans started hunting them.

Today many of the last megafauna may go extinct unless we help them.

Future experiment ➡ How do we stop megafauna going extinct like the dinosaurs?

BRONTOTHERIUM

(Bron-toe-THEE-ree-um)
Means "Thunder Beast"

PREHISTORIC MAMMALS

132

318 Million	299 Million	252 Million	201 Million	14
PENNSYL-VANIAN	PERMIAN	TRIASSIC	JURASSIC	

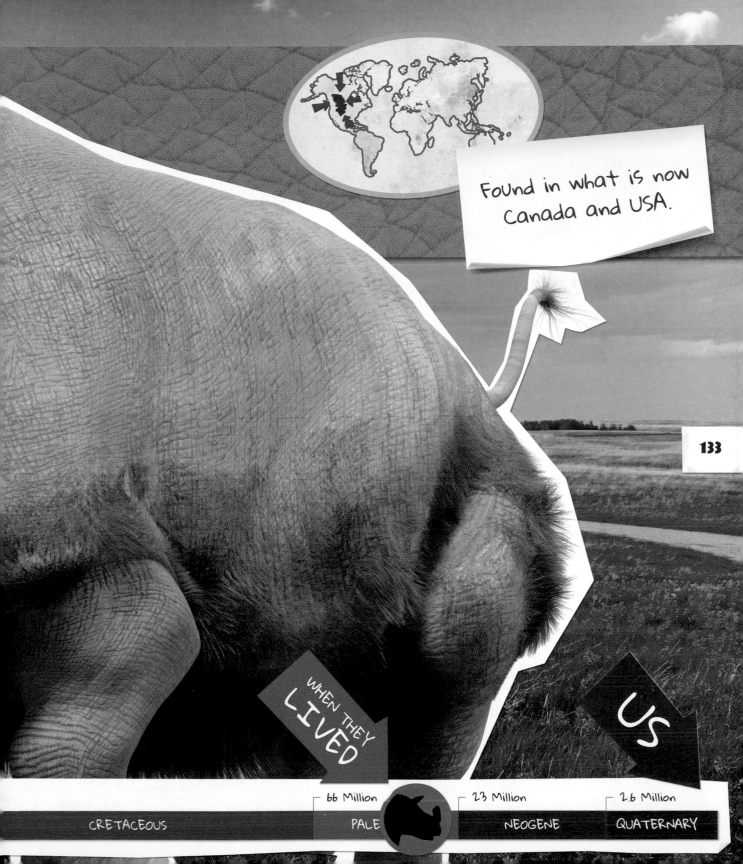

BRONTOTHERIUM

Both girls and boys had horns, but boys had bigger ones.

★ Weighed as much as five horses!

134

★ In the same family as prehistoric horses.

Brontotherium and Megacerops are the same animal.

Most paleontologsts use the name Megacerops which means Big Horned Face.

fought with other Brontotheriums over mates.

Like rhinos today!

Y-shaped horn on its nose.

Brontotherium horns are made of solid bone.

Rhinos' horns are made of keratin like our fingernails.

Me vs. Bronto

As long as a tractor.

QUESTION: How does the Brontotherium attract a mate?

BACKGROUND RESEARCH NOTES:

★ Brontotherium means "Thunder Beast"

★ It looks like a rhino, but it's a prehistoric relative of the horse

★ The Brontotherium has a Y-shaped horn, and boys have longer horns than girls.

MY PLAN:

Observe a male and female Brontotherium in my yard to see if they become mates.

FIELD NOTES:

1. The male Brontotherium called out to the female Brontotherium by making loud noises.
   » Update = The female Brontotherium left, calling wasn't enough to attract her!

FIELD NOTES (CONTINUED):

2. Next, the male Bronto stomped his feet, did some showing off, and it looks like he smiled at the girl Brototherium!

   » Update = Uh oh. She left again, the male needs to do more if he wants her to stay!

3. This time, the male Bronto made low, rumbling noises at the female Bronto.

   » Update = It worked! She responded with some rumbles of her own. She's staying and now they're nuzzling and listening to each other!

FINDING:

The male Brontotherium tried to attract the female Brontotherium by calling, stomping his feet and showing off, BUT what worked best was talking and listening—in Bronto rumbles!

WOOLLY MAMMOTH

 (Wool-ly Mam-moth)
Means "Hairy and Extremely Large"

Found in what is now North America, Europe, and Asia.

138

⌐318 Million	⌐299 Million	⌐252 Million	⌐201 Million	
PENNSYL-VANIAN	PERMIAN	TRIASSIC	JURASSIC	

139

Lived at the same time as people!

WHEN THEY LIVED

US

| 66 Million | 23 Million | 2.6 |
| CRETACEOUS | PALEOGENE | NEOGENE | Q |

WOOLLY MAMMOTH

One of the oldest known musical instruments is a flute made out of a mammoth tusk.

What's the difference between a tusk and a horn?

★ Was as long and weighed as much as an African elephant.

★ Went extinct only 4,000 years ago!

Horns are at the top of an animal's head, tusks are large teeth that come from their mouths.

Scientists can tell how old they were by the rings in their tusks.

Tusks were used for defense, to impress mates, and to clear snow to find food.

Tusks

were as long as three of me!

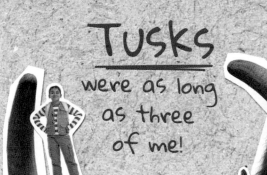

Me vs. Mammoth

Had humps on its back.

DINO EXPERIMENT 616

QUESTION: What was it like for cave people to live with the Woolly Mammoth?

BACKGROUND RESEARCH NOTES:

I did research at the museum, used my imagination, and made drawings to figure this out!

(Dad, Saara and I didn't really go back in time to see the Woolly Mammoth...I wish!)

MY PLAN:

Learn from Woolly Mammoth fossils at the museum and then tell a story about what it would be like to be part of a cave person family at the same time as Mammoths!

FIELD NOTES:

1. Looking at fossils at the museum, I got the idea to draw a picture of the Woolly Mammoth just like cave kids did. Then I decided to tell Dad and Saara a story about how cave dads and their kids hunted mammoths with wooden spears!

FIELD NOTES (CONTINUED):

2. But Woolly Mammoths were tough for cave people to hunt because they were huge and defended themselves with their massive tusks.

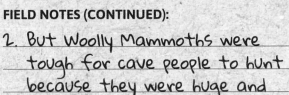

3. Then I remembered that the Smilodon hunted both cave people and mammoths! Uh oh, I see a Smilodon coming!

FINDING:

Cave people drew paintings of the Woolly Mammoth and hunted them with wooden spears but Woolly Mammoths defended themselves against cave people and Smilodons!

BABY WOOLLY MAMMOTH

PREHISTORIC MAMMALS

Baby mammoths could grow up to be eighty years old!

318 Million	299 Million		252 Million		201 Million	
PENNSYL-VANIAN	PERMIAN		TRIASSIC		JURASSIC	

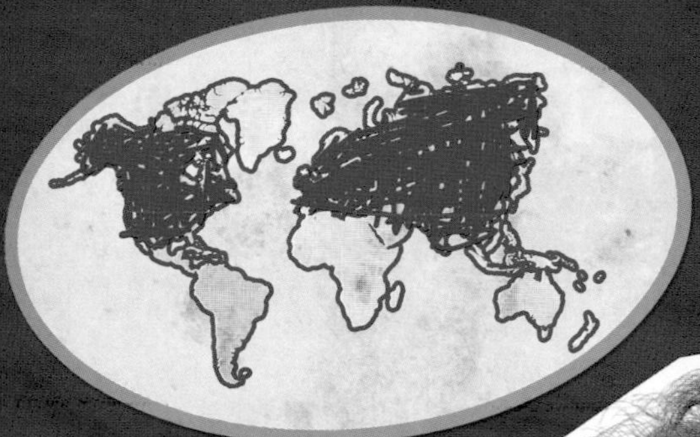

Found in what is now North America, Europe and Asia.

WHEN THEY LIVED

US

| | 66 Million | 23 Million | 2.6 |
| CRETACEOUS | PALEOGENE | NEOGENE | QU |

DINO EXPERIMENT __812__

QUESTION: What do mammoths use their trunks for?

BACKGROUND RESEARCH NOTES:

★ Mom mammoths feed their babies milk, just like humans and elephants.

★ Mammoth babies start to grow their first set of tusks when they are just six months old.

MY PLAN:

Observe a mom and baby mammoth in my yard to see how they use their trunks.

FIELD NOTES:

1. I see an ADORABLE mammoth baby in my yard. She just fell down, and she sucked on her trunk to comfort herself! Soooooo cute.

2. I tried to get closer to the baby, but her mom thought I was a predator and used her trunk to MOVE the baby away.
   » Update = I need to become a mammoth baby if I'm going to learn more. It's Mammoth Time!

FIELD NOTES (CONTINUED):

3. Now that I'm a mammoth, the mom and baby have accepted me into their herd! They used their trunks to SMELL me and TRUMPET a hello!

4. Experiment back on! While I was feeding Dex, the mom mammoth used her trunk like a straw and SUCKED up all the water in our sink and SPRAYED the water into her mouth and her baby's mouth too. But she also sprayed some water on my field guide...

FINDING:

Mammoth trunks are amazing! They use their trunks for:
- » Comfort
- » Moving things (like food!)
- » Smelling
- » Trumpeting
- » Sucking up and spraying water

SMILODON

PREHISTORIC MAMMALS

(Smile-oh-don)
Means "knife tooth"

Because their teeth were as sharp as knives!

318 Million	299 Million	252 Million	201 Million	14
PENNSYL-VANIAN	PERMIAN	TRIASSIC	JURASSIC	

Lived in what is now North and South America.

151

WHEN THEY LIVED

US

SMILODON

★ Weighed as much as but was a little smaller than a lion.

152

...which means they may have caught their prey by dropping down on them from above—making it an ambush predator like many cats today.

Ambush predator means they would wait and then surprise their prey.

130,000 Smilodon bones have been found at the La Brea Tar Pits in Los Angeles.

Front teeth were as long as Saara's head.

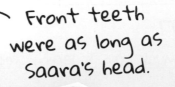

Also called a saber-toothed cat because their front teeth looked like sabres.

Smilodon is most famous for its relatively long canines, which are the longest found in the saber-toothed cats.

Canines are teeth that are sharp and pointy. Perfect for tearing food!

Me vs. Smilodon

Lived at the same time as cave people.

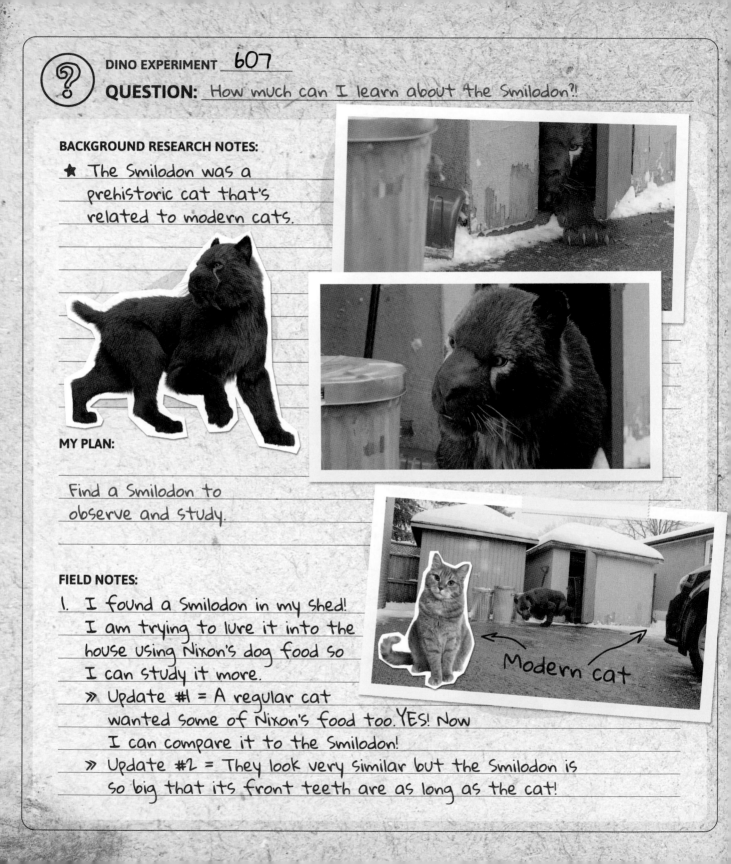

DINO EXPERIMENT __607__

QUESTION: How much can I learn about the Smilodon?!

BACKGROUND RESEARCH NOTES:

★ The Smilodon was a prehistoric cat that's related to modern cats.

MY PLAN:

Find a Smilodon to observe and study.

FIELD NOTES:

1. I found a Smilodon in my shed! I am trying to lure it into the house using Nixon's dog food so I can study it more.

   » Update #1 = A regular cat wanted some of Nixon's food too. YES! Now I can compare it to the Smilodon!

   » Update #2 = They look very similar but the Smilodon is so big that its front teeth are as long as the cat!

Modern cat

FIELD NOTES (CONTINUED):

2. Mom found me and said I couldn't bring a wild animal into our house.

3. Uh oh... the Smilodon got in anyways and he's now in my room!! I need to find a way to get him out.

4. He ate Saara's camel stuffie! Yikes.
   » Update #1 = That's it! Smilodon must hunt camels! I'll dress Nixon up like a camel to get the Smilodon out, then run back inside.
   » Update #2 = It worked... The Smilodon is outside and Nixon is safe... But Saara isn't happy about her camel getting destroyed....

Sorry seester! !!

FINDING:

The Smilodon is a massive cat with huge teeth that hunts camels! I can't wait to learn more!

Lived in what is now North and South America.

157

WHEN THEY LIVED

US

66 Million

23 Million

CRETACEOUS

PALEOGENE

NEOGENE

RY

BABY SMILODON

Had a short tail like a Bobcat.

158

Fossils of Smilodon have been found together meaning they probably lived in prides—like lions do today.

A pride is what a group of lions is called.

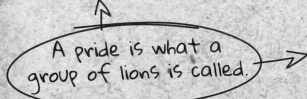

Like people, their adult teeth pushed out their baby teeth.

⟮ EXCEPT ⟯

Sometimes Smilodon babies had both teeth at the same time.

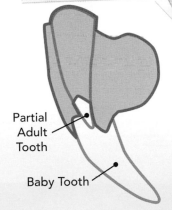

Partial Adult Tooth

Baby Tooth

Me vs. Baby Smilodon

TEETH WERE SO BIG THEIR LIPS COULDN'T COVER THEM.

Which means they might have drooled like my brother Dex!

DINO EXPERIMENT 607

QUESTION: How do Smilodon families live?

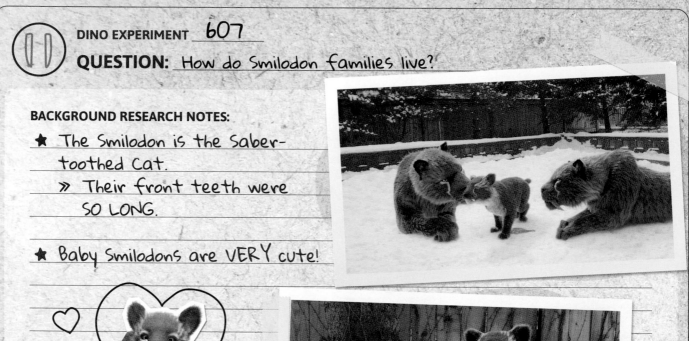

BACKGROUND RESEARCH NOTES:

★ The Smilodon is the Saber-toothed Cat.
  » Their front teeth were SO LONG.

★ Baby Smilodons are VERY cute!

MY PLAN:

Find a baby Smilodon and its parents to see how they all lived as a family!

FIELD NOTES:

1. I found a baby Smilodon outside! He is SO CUTE! I have to stay in scientist mode and not get too attached to my subject... Just observe... No petting... This will be hard!

FIELD NOTES (CONTINUED):

2. ~~The mom just came and she brought the little baby some lunch! So cute!~~
   The female Smilodon appears to have brought her offspring some food.

3. Oh no! A Nanuqsaurus is coming to eat the baby Smilodon, and I don't know where his mom went! Watch out baby!
   » Update #1 = Phew! Now the dad Smilodon is here to scare off the Nanuq!
   » Update #2 = And the mom just came back with more fish!
   » Update #3 = Now that the baby is safe I just had to pet him... (I'm a scientist but I also love cute babies!).

FINDING:

The mom and dad Smilodon both take care of their baby but in different ways. The mom hunts for food and the dad protects them.

TERROR BIRDS

TERROR BIRDS

Terror birds first appeared 62 million years ago.

Four million years after the dinosaurs went extinct.

It's believed that terror birds got so big by hunting mammals.

Like prehistoric horses!

They were called Terror Birds because they had sharp talons on their feet and powerful beaks that can snap a bone in half!

TITANIS

(Tie-tan-is)
Means "Giant"

TERROR BIRDS

166

318 Million	299 Million		252 Million		201 Million	
PENNSYL-VANIAN	PERMIAN		TRIASSIC		JURASSIC	

Found in what is now Florida and Texas, USA.

WHEN THEY LIVED

US

	66 Million		23 Million		2.6 Million
CRETACEOUS		PALEOGENE		NEOG	QUATERNARY

TITANIS

IT COULD RUN FASTER THAN A HORSE.

↑
Which is helpful because it hunted them.

★ Could grow taller than my Dad and weigh more than my Mom.

Had a hook at the end of its beak to help it tear off meat

Had wings but they were too small to let it fly.

Me vs. Titanis

Could have used its strong legs to kick its prey.

169

DINO EXPERIMENT **7|6**

QUESTION: How do terror birds hunt?

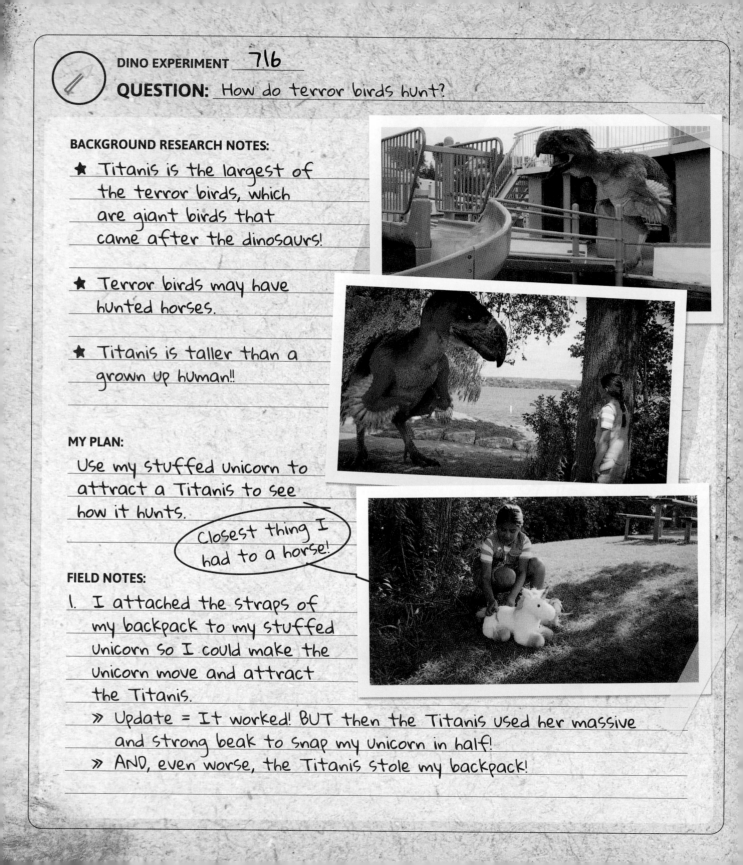

BACKGROUND RESEARCH NOTES:

★ Titanis is the largest of the terror birds, which are giant birds that came after the dinosaurs!

★ Terror birds may have hunted horses.

★ Titanis is taller than a grown up human!!

MY PLAN:

Use my stuffed unicorn to attract a Titanis to see how it hunts.

Closest thing I had to a horse!

FIELD NOTES:

1. I attached the straps of my backpack to my stuffed unicorn so I could make the unicorn move and attract the Titanis.

   » Update = It worked! BUT then the Titanis used her massive and strong beak to snap my unicorn in half!

   » AND, even worse, the Titanis stole my backpack!

FIELD NOTES (CONTINUED):

2. I got a police officer to help me track down the Titanis.

   » Update #1 = I found the Titanis, and she used her claws to rip up my backpack. Now I know terror birds also use their sharp claws to hunt. But she still has my backpack!

   » Update #2 = Guess what?! This police officer is Dan and Trek's mom! AND she made the field guide!!! SO COOL!

3. We called Dan for advice on how to slow down the terror bird so we could catch up—he told us to give her beef jerky!

   » Update = It worked! I got my backpack back and saw that the Titanis used her powerful neck to shake her prey! Amazing!

FINDING:

Terror birds used three things to help them hunt:

   » Massive beak to break bones.
   » Sharp claws to tear things apart.
   » Powerful neck to shake its prey.

PREHISTORIC SNAKES

PREHISTORIC SNAKES

Snakes first slithered around the dinosaurs starting between 143 and 167 million years ago.

Which means some prehistoric snakes ate dinosaurs!

Dinosaurs and prehistoric snakes hunted each other. A fossil was discovered in India of a snake attacking a newly hatched dinosaur in its nest.

All snakes have these things in common:

» They have forked tongues.

» They eat meat.

» They have no arms or legs.

» That are shaped like a tube.

» They are super flexible.

» They have scales.

» They are cold-blooded.

Cold-blooded animals get their body heat from their environments. So if it's cold, they're cold and if it's hot, they're hot.

Like the Titanoboa!

After the dinosaurs became extinct 66 million years ago, lots of different snakes appeared on Earth.

Snakes are always growing, but the temperature of where they live impacts their growth.

The hotter it is outside, the bigger the snake.

WHICH MEANS

As the world cooled, prehistoric snakes got smaller.

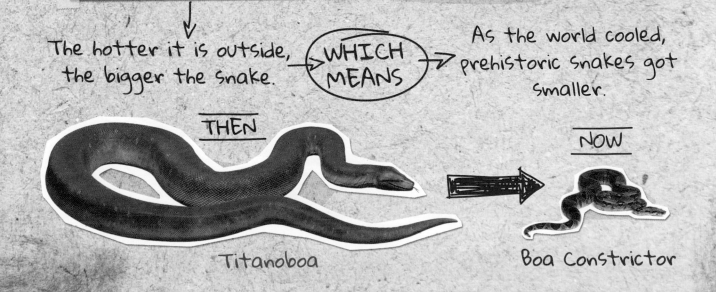

THEN

NOW

Titanoboa

Boa Constrictor

TITANOBOA

PREHISTORIC SNAKES

(Tie-tan-O-Boa)
Means "Titanic Boa"

176

318 Million	299 Million		252 Million		201 Million		14*
PENNSYL-VANIAN	PERMIAN		TRIASSIC			JURASSIC	

Found in what is now Colombia.

177

WHEN THEY LIVED

US

CRETACEOUS			NEOGENE	QUATERNARY
	66 Million		23 Million	2.6 Million

TITANOBOA

Mostly lived in the water.

Titanoboa was a constrictor.

★ Was as long as a transport truck.

★ Weighed as much as two grand pianos.

3 ways snakes catch their prey:

1 Constricting their prey, which means they wrap around their prey until they can't breath anymore.

2 Biting venomously, which means they give poison through a bite.

3 Eating them alive.

Like snakes today, it had a forked tongue that it used to smell.

Might have only eaten once a year!

Why?

Didn't need as much energy.

Ate bigger meals that took longer to digest.

Biggest, longest, and heaviest snake ever discovered! The biggest snake today is the Green Anaconda.

Me vs. Titano

With no dinosaurs around, Titanoboa was the largest predator on Earth before it became extinct.

DINO EXPERIMENT ___511___

QUESTION: Was the Titanoboa venomous or a constrictor?

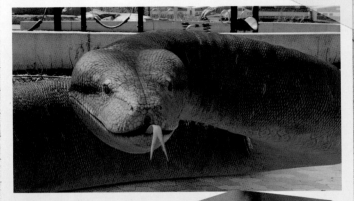

BACKGROUND RESEARCH NOTES:

★ Venomous snakes get their prey by biting them with their fangs, which are very pointy teeth in the front, and injecting them with venom.

★ Constrictor snakes don't have venom or fangs. Instead they grab their prey and wrap around it and squeeze.

Fangs

No fangs

MY PLAN:

Observe a Titanoboa to see if it has fangs or not. If it does, that means it's venomous!

FIELD NOTES:

1. I hissed at the Titanoboa to get her to open her mouth, but instead she just LICKED me! Ew!

   » Update = Mom says the Titanoboa smells for prey by licking... so maybe she's hunting for prey!

FIELD NOTES (CONTINUED):

If she bites her prey, then I'll know she's venomous.

If she wraps around her prey then she's a constrictor and not venomous!

2. I see a T. rex! Maybe the Titanoboa will go after him... I'll lead the T. rex over to the Titanoboa with some jerky.
   » Update = The Titanoboa is wrapping herself around the T. rex! She also hissed and I could see there were no fangs. That means she's a constrictor and NOT venomous!

FINDING:

The Titanoboa is NOT venomous. It's a constrictor and does not have fangs, which means it wraps itself around its prey to squeeze it instead of biting it.

PREHISTORIC INSECTS

PREHISTORIC INSECTS

Insects appeared 182 million years BEFORE the dinosaurs!

They've been around for over 412 million years!

Insects are one of the oldest and most successful forms of life on the planet.

Why?

Because there are so many of them. Scientists believe there are over 10 quintillion individual insects alive today.

That's this many zeroes:
10,000,000,000,000,000,000!

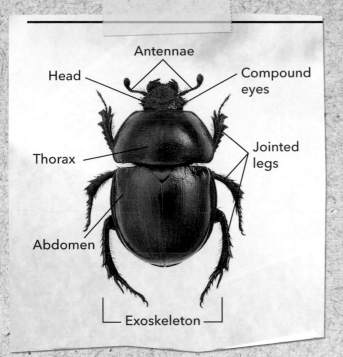

Antennae

Head

Compound eyes

Jointed legs

Thorax

Abdomen

Exoskeleton

All insects have these things in common:

- They all have a hard shell. (called an exoskeleton)
- They have a three-part body. (Head, Thorax, Abdomen)
- They all have three pairs of legs.
- They have one pair of antennae.
- They all have compound eyes.

Compound eyes look like this:

WHEN THEY FIRST APPEARED, INSECTS WERE SMALL BUT THEY GOT BIG FAST.

Why?

They were able to grow so big because at the time there was more oxygen in the air.

More oxygen meant that insects could get more air and grow bigger.

That's what we breathe too!

MEGANEURA

(Meg-ah-neur-ah)
Means "Large veined"

Because they had vein patterns in their wings.

186

First discovered in what is now France.

WHEN THEY LIVED

┌ 299 Million   ┌ 252 Million   ┌ 201 Million   ┌ 1

PERMIAN   TRIASSIC   JURASSIC

US

66 Million

23 Million

2.6 Million

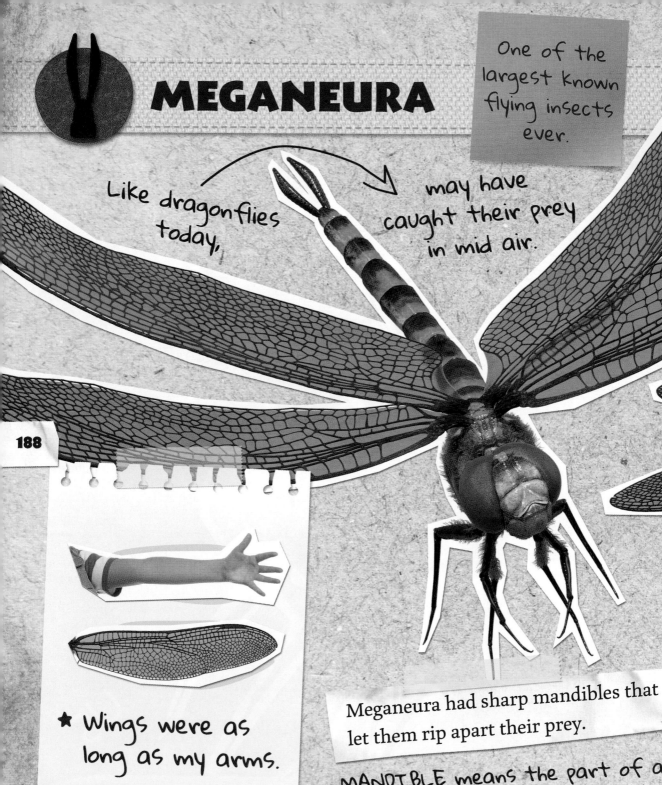

MEGANEURA

188

One of the largest known flying insects ever.

Like dragonflies today,

may have caught their prey in mid air.

★ Wings were as long as my arms.

Meganeura had sharp mandibles that let them rip apart their prey.

MANDIBLE means the part of an insect's mouth that it uses to bite.

Had two pairs of wings which let them fly in all directions and even hover like a helicopter!

Had incredible eyesight!

Could see in front and behind at the same time!

Lived before pterosaurs, birds, and bats ever existed.

Me vs. Meganeura

Looked like dragonflies, but much, much, much bigger!

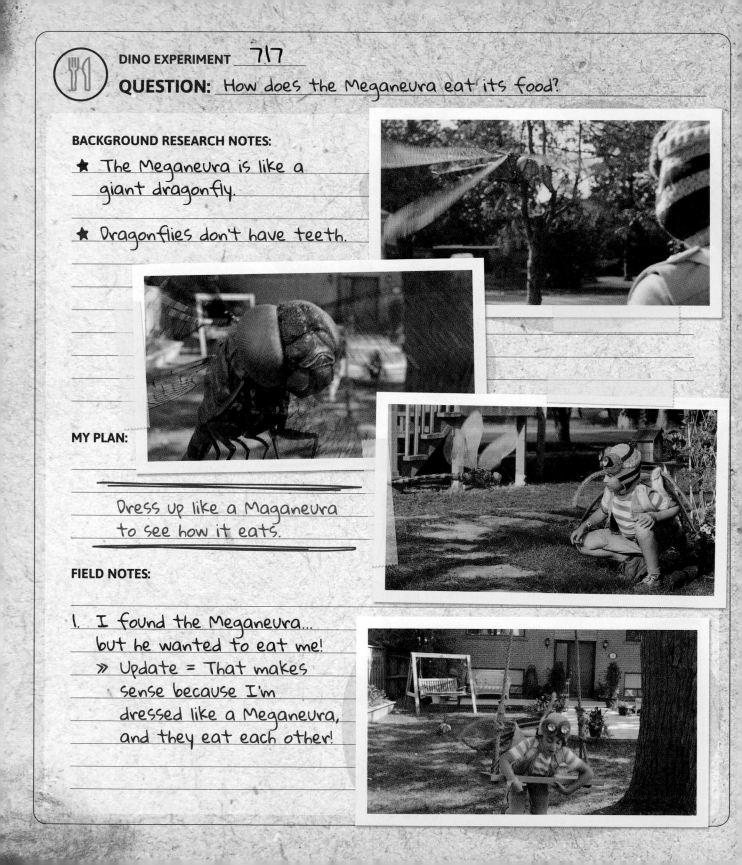

DINO EXPERIMENT __7|7__

QUESTION: How does the Meganeura eat its food?

BACKGROUND RESEARCH NOTES:

★ The Meganeura is like a giant dragonfly.

★ Dragonflies don't have teeth.

MY PLAN:

Dress up like a Maganeura to see how it eats.

FIELD NOTES:

1. I found the Meganeura... but he wanted to eat me!
   » Update = That makes sense because I'm dressed like a Meganeura, and they eat each other!

FIELD NOTES (CONTINUED):

2. I took my costume off so he wouldn't snack on me, and I attached some beef jerky to Dexter's toy lizard to use as bait.

Thanks Dex!!

   » Update = The Meganeura flew by so <u>fast</u> to grab the jerky (and the lizard) that I could hardly see it!

> They can fly almost as fast as a cheetah can run!

3. Mom had the best idea! Meganeura lived by water, so we made the bathtub into a pond! Now I can finish my experiment.

   » Update #1 = The Meganeura came back—AND brought Dexter's lizard! Phew.
   » Update #2 = The Meganeura is chewing the jerky using his two strong (mandibles), just like dragonflies!

> More like observational research, technically!

> Mandibles are outside the mouth and can be used instead of teeth to crunch up food!

FINDING:

The Meganeura uses the two strong mandibles outside of its mouth to crunch up its food since it didn't have teeth!

HUMAN EYES vs MEGANEURA EYES

Human eyes

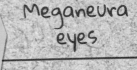
Meganeura eyes

LENSES
Meganeura has 30,000 lenses that pick up light from different directions.

People only have one lens in each eye!

☆☆☆ Round 1 Meganeura WINS! ☆☆☆

CLOSE vs FAR
Meganeura focus on DISTANT objects.
Human eyes focus on CLOSE objects.

≠ ≠ ≠ Round 2 TIE! ≠ ≠ ≠

Meganeura has nearly 360 degree vision.

People only have 120 degree vision.

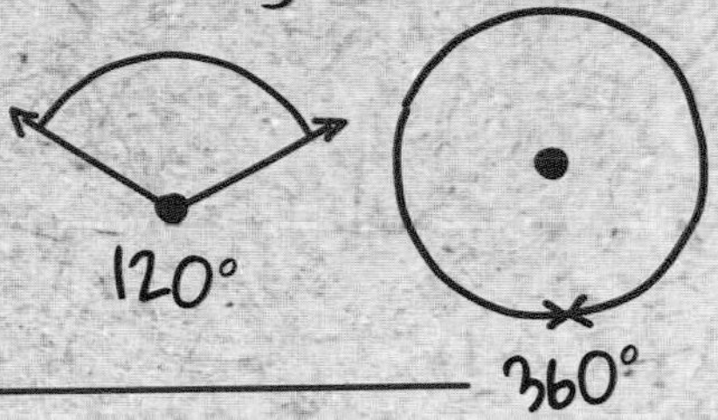

120°

360°

☆ ☆ ☆ Round 3 Meganeura WINS! ☆ ☆ ☆

SPEED LIMIT 200

Meganeura see 200 images per second.

We only see 60 images per second.

☆ ☆ ☆ Round 4 Meganeura WINS! ☆ ☆ ☆

☆ ☆ ☆ SCORECARD ☆ ☆ ☆

3.5 to 0.5

MEGANEURA has better eyesight than people!

DINO EXPERIMENT 520

QUESTION: Which Dinosaur ^(or prehistoric creature) had the best eyesight for hunting?

BACKGROUND RESEARCH NOTES:

★ The Nanuqsaurus lived up north where it's dark half of the year, so it's possible it could see well in the dark!

★ Some paleontologists think the T. rex could see like an eagle, which is like looking through binoculars.

(Makes sense because birds came from dinosaurs!)

MY PLAN:

Observe different dinosaurs chasing the Compsognathus as prey! Good thing I'm at the eye doctor's today for expert sight advice!

FIELD NOTES:

1. The Compy is too speedy for the Nanuq. Sorry Nanuq—you don't win for best eyesight for hunting... maybe at night time!

FIELD NOTES (CONTINUED):

2. The T. rex could see the Compy from far away! But the Compy was too sneaky and camouflaged itself!

3. Dr. Webster had a great idea... an animal with heat vision would be able to spot the Compy even when it's camouflaged, because it lets you see the heat coming off of a body!
No dinosaurs had heat vision, but the Titanoboa did!
» Update = The heat vision worked and the Titanoboa was able to capture the Compy! (Thanks to Dr. Webster's heat vision goggles!)

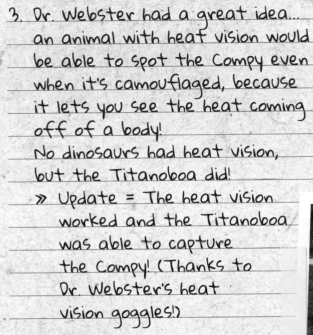

FINDING:

It wasn't a dinosaur that had the best eyesight for hunting... it was the Titanoboa! A prehistoric snake with super-hot heat vision!

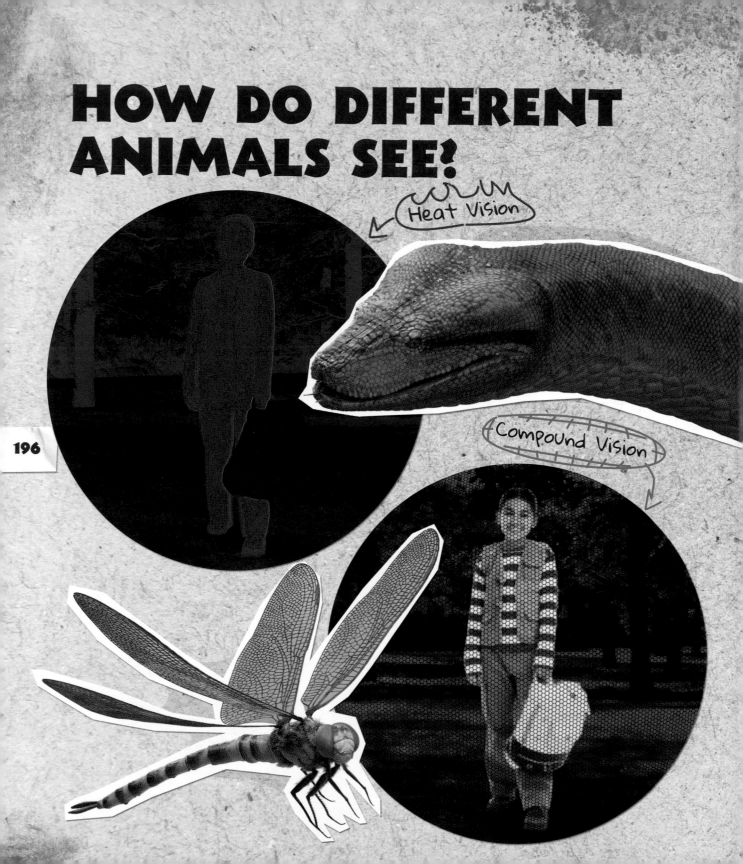

HOW DO DIFFERENT ANIMALS SEE?

Heat Vision

Compound Vision

PHOTO GLOSSARY

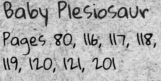

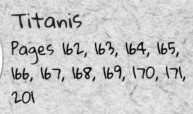

ABOUT THE AUTHORS

My friends helped me write this guide.

J.J. JOHNSON

J.J. is a multi-Emmy award-winning executive producer, director, writer, and the creator of *Dino Dan*, *Dino Dan: Trek's Adventures* and *Dino Dana*. His top three favorite prehistoric creatures are the Megalodon, the Quetzalcoatlus and the Titanis.

CHRISTIN SIMMS

Christin is an Emmy award-winning executive producer and writer. Her favorite prehistoric creature is the Baby Mammoth.

COLLEEN RUSSO JOHNSON, PHD

Colleen is the director of research at Sinking Ship Entertainment which means she figures out ways to make things fun and educational. Her favorite prehistoric creature is the Baby Smilodon.

Here are some photos of us!